A HEART
FOR GOD

THE CHRISTIAN CHARACTER LIBRARY aims to help Christians live out the biblical mandate to become "salt" and "light" in our world through the witness of Christlike character.

In its radical essence, Christian character is not an accumulation of personal virtues, nor is it a lifestyle—it is a life. It is the life of the risen, living Lord Jesus who expresses His nature through us as we surrender our hearts and lives to Him daily.

As we study His life in the Scriptures and commune with Him in prayer, He removes the veil of our sin-darkened nature and transforms us into His own likeness with ever-increasing glory.

The books in The Christian Character Library have been written with the purpose of encouraging you to model the character of our Lord Jesus Christ in a way that bears fruit in the lives of other people—through the power of a life that reflects "Christ in you, the hope of glory."

A HEART FOR GOD

SINCLAIR B. FERGUSON

THE CHRISTIAN CHARACTER LIBRARY

NAVPRESS

A MINISTRY OF THE NAVIGATORS
P.O. Box 6000, Colorado Springs, Colorado 80934

The Navigators is an international Christian organization. Jesus Christ gave His followers the Great Commission to go and make disciples (Matthew 28:19). The aim of The Navigators is to help fulfill that commission by multiplying laborers for Christ in every nation.

NavPress is the publishing ministry of The Navigators. NavPress publications are tools to help Christians grow. Although publications alone cannot make disciples or change lives, they can help believers learn biblical discipleship, and apply what they learn to their lives and ministries.

© 1985 by Sinclair B. Ferguson
All rights reserved, including translation
Library of Congress Catalog Card Number:
    85-061282
ISBN: 0-89109-507-1
15073

Second printing, 1986

Unless otherwise identified, all Scripture quotations in the publication are from the *Holy Bible: New International Version* (NIV). Copyright © 1973, 1978, 1984, International Bible Society. Used by permission of Zondervan Bible Publishers.

Printed in the United States of America

Contents

Author

Sinclair B. Ferguson is Associate Professor of Systematic Theology at Westminster Theological Seminary in Philadelphia, Pennsylvania. He was born in Scotland and served as a pastor in Glasgow and on the Island of Unst, in the Shetland Isles, some 150 miles north of the mainland of Scotland. He holds degrees in Philosophy and Theology from the University of Aberdeen, including a Ph.D.

He and his wife, Dorothy, have four children: David, Peter, John, and Ruth.

Other books by Sinclair Ferguson:

> *Discovering God's Will* (Banner of Truth, 1981)
>
> *Know Your Christian Life* (InterVarsity, 1981)
>
> *Taking the Christian Life Seriously* (Zondervan, 1981)
>
> *Man Overboard: A Study of the Life of Jonah* (Tyndale, 1982)
>
> *Grow in Grace* (NavPress, 1984)

To
William Still
in deep gratitude

Preface

Since I was a little boy nothing has fascinated me more than the knowledge of God: Who is God? Can God be known? If He can be known, how do we discover Him? Now, in later years, I realize that these are not merely questions of childhood; they are the most important questions in the universe. Moreover, they lie at the heart of the Christian faith. Christians today do not always see that as clearly as they should. Perhaps that explains why we are not all that we ought to be, either in our worship in the church or in our witness to the world. My hope is that these pages will contribute, in some way, to more God-centered living.

For this reason, *A Heart for God* is oriented towards biblical exposition. It is only as Christ's words remain in us and we remain in Him that we will be delivered from the rootless Christianity so characteristic of our times. As His Word influences us, we begin to bear fruit and prove to be His disciples (John 15:5-8). Only as God's Word impacts the way we think, live, and feel will we develop hearts that are characterized by obedience to God and filled with love for Him.

I send this book out both nervously and prayerfully. Nervously, because of the vastness and sheer glory of the subject, and a deep consciousness of my own inadequacy rightly to write about the God whom I have come to love and in some measure know. Prayerfully, because I have tried to present the teaching He has given us in Scripture, and I long with all my heart that He might use that to help you to know Him. These pages come to you with the request that you too read them prayerfully, with an increasing desire to grow in the knowledge of God.

+ + +

I would like to express my gratitude to the staff of NavPress for their encouragement to me to write, and especially to Don Simpson and Kathy Yanni, who have become special friends. Only those who know me personally will appreciate the extent to which the writing of these pages has depended on the love of my wife, Dorothy, and our four children: David, Peter, John, and Ruth. I hope they will all feel both thanked and hugged!

SINCLAIR B. FERGUSON

Day by day, dear Lord, of Thee three things I pray:
  To see Thee more clearly
  To love Thee more dearly
  To follow Thee more nearly.

(Prayer of Richard of Chichester, 1197-1253)

1
Growing in the Knowledge of God

What is the most important thing in the world to every Christian? It is to grow in the knowledge of God.

The knowledge of God is the heart of salvation and all true spiritual experience. Knowing Him is what we were created for. It will occupy us throughout all eternity. In Scripture, it is almost equivalent to salvation. Jesus said that eternal life, or salvation, means knowledge of God: "Now this is eternal life: that they may know you, the only true God, and Jesus Christ, whom you have sent" (John 17:3). To be a Christian is not a *mindless* experience, but involves knowledge and understanding. It means a personal relationship and personal acquaintance with the Lord.

Behind what Jesus says in John's Gospel lies the promise that God gave centuries before in the prophecy of the new covenant: "I will give them a heart to know me, that I am the LORD" (Jeremiah 24:7). The fulfillment of that prophecy would mean, Jeremiah added, "No longer will a man teach his neighbor, or a man his brother, saying, 'Know the LORD,' because they will all know me, from the least of them to the greatest" (Jeremiah 31:34). Isaiah similarly tells us that this knowledge of God is what would mark the reign of the promised Messiah, Jesus Christ: "the earth will be full of the knowledge of the LORD as the waters cover the sea" (Isaiah 11:9). What a vision! And yet it summarizes what Scripture tells us Christ came to do: to bring us the knowledge of God.

Such knowledge of God is really the heart of all true understanding in the Christian life. A man or woman may be a Christian and remain ignorant of many things. But we cannot be Christians and remain ignorant of God. In the final analysis, says the wise man in Proverbs, "knowledge of the Holy One is understanding" (9:10). While man has never had so much knowledge about the world as he possesses today, perhaps he has never had so little knowledge of God. That is why our times are marked by a singular lack of understanding, appreciation, and genuine insight into the need of the hour.

Scripture also teaches us that the knowledge of God is a great preservative from sin. Isaiah shares in the divine lament over Israel and her rebellion when he says, "The ox knows his master, the donkey his owner's manger, but Israel does not know, my people do not understand" (Isaiah 1:3). The root cause of their spiritual decline is their lack of understanding.

When people truly know God and are growing in a genuine relationship with Him, however, their lives are marked by integrity and reliability. They do not treat dishonesty of the heart or of the lips indifferently. They are, in a word, *holy.* But our age is frightened of holiness. It's all the more tragic, therefore, that the church has also become frightened of holiness. It likes nothing less than to be different. The same may be true of us individually. Why? Because we do not know God as we should. If we really knew Him, it would show in the character of our lives.

The knowledge of God is also essential to Christian growth. In the opening section of Peter's second letter, he draws attention to this crucial fact. He urges his friends to grow spiritually, wishing them grace and peace "through the knowledge of God." He tells them that God's power has given us everything we need to live the Christian life "through our knowledge of him who called us by his own glory and goodness" (2 Peter 1:2-3). Similarly, when Paul expresses his desire for the Christians at Colosse to grow spiritually, the same theme recurs: Growth is particularly accompanied by "growing in the knowledge of God" (Colossians 1:10).

Our mistake has been to compose our *own* ground rules for the Christian life—how presumptuous can we be?—instead of listening to what God Himself wants to say to us, namely: "If you want to grow as a Christian, you must first of all grow in the knowledge of Me."

+   +   +

This knowledge of God is our greatest privilege. Hear Jeremiah again: "This is what the LORD says: 'Let not the wise man boast of his wisdom or the strong man boast of his strength or the rich man boast of his riches, but let him who boasts boast about this: that he understands and knows me, that I am the LORD, who exercises kindness, justice and righteousness on earth, for in these I delight,' declares the LORD" (Jeremiah 9:23-24). This declaration is from the same man whose speech had begun with, "Oh, that my head were a spring of water and my eyes a fountain of tears . . ." (Jeremiah 9:1). No ivory-tower theologian or author was Jeremiah! Here was a man suffering for the sake of his people, seeing things with the clarity of one who was an outsider in every society, except in the society of God. He penetrated through all the superficialities of life to the heart of the matter. Who cares for the wisdom of this world, or the strength of men, or the riches and fame some attain, if all these things are to be had without knowing God? With devastating honesty, Jeremiah reduced all these things men desire to their proper (and very secondary place) in his "Jeremiad." Life is only worth boasting about if at its center is the knowledge of God, controlling all our aspirations. That *is* something to boast about.

What do you and I boast about? What subject

of conversation most arouses us and fills our hearts? Do we consider knowing God to be the greatest treasure in the world, and by far our greatest privilege? If not, we are but pygmies in the world of the spirit. We have sold our Christian birthright for a mess of pottage, and our true Christian experience will be superficial, inadequate, and tragically out of focus.

Unfortunately, many of our Christian lives are suffering from such spiritual astigmatism. It shows in our personal lives; it shows in our dealings with others; it shows in our lack of impact on the world; it shows perhaps most obviously in the character of our worship. This was what Jeremiah saw in his time. No wonder he wept! No wonder there were moments when he had to fight off the depths of depression—because he too was bound up with the people. He could not castigate them without feeling the blows himself.

How sensitive are you to this issue? Knowing God is your single greatest privilege as a Christian, and the one that sensitizes you to every other issue of importance. But is this the issue that lies at the center of *your* thinking?

+   +   +

When we look back on what the masters of the spiritual life have written and said, it's hard to escape the conclusion that we have been the victim of a confidence trick in our century. Over the past few decades, the evangelical church has been gripped by a series of issues and concerns that have primarily been marginal, or at best of secondary importance. Conferences, seminars, and books on a whole series of "vital concerns" have dominated center stage and determined the agenda in many churches and for many individual Christians. *But strikingly absent has been concentration on God Himself.* Indeed, on the rare occasions when this absence has not been the case, we have sat up to take notice as though something out of the ordinary were being said! What has happened, in effect, is that we have redefined the Christian life and the meaning of eternal life in terms of any number of particular issues. We have not listened to the insistent voice of Jesus Christ telling us that it means the knowledge of God.

What is involved in "growing in the knowledge of God"? This phrase appears in Paul's description of his continual prayer for the Colossians. The content of Paul's prayer has a great deal to teach us about basic principles of growth in knowing the Lord:

> We have not stopped praying for you and asking God to fill you with the knowledge of his will through all spiritual wisdom and understanding. And we pray this in order that you may live a life worthy of the Lord and may please him in every way: bearing fruit in every good work, growing in the knowledge of God, being strengthened with all power according to his glorious might so that you may have great endurance and patience. . . . (Colossians 1:9-11)

Paul suggests in this passage that there are

four fundamental "laws" governing the knowledge of God in the growing believer:

1. *God alone is the author of our knowledge of Himself.* One of the great writers of the early Christian church, Hilary of Poitiers, echoed this truth: "God alone is a fit witness to Himself." No one less than God can bring us true and reliable knowledge about Him: God must give it Himself. This is why Paul is not content to instruct the Colossians by simply informing them about God. He *prays* for them, asking that *God* will teach them about Himself.

This is a most humbling truth. Here I am, with all my knowledge and education. I know so much! Yet before God, I am a beginner who depends upon the Holy Spirit to be my teacher and guide. Paul says elsewhere that the Holy Spirit alone knows the thoughts of God and searches the "deep things" of God (1 Corinthians 2:10-11). The marvel of His witness and ministry to us is that He reveals the heart of God to us. "We have not received the spirit of the world [which is incapable of understanding and loving God]," writes Paul, "but the Spirit who is from God, that we may understand what God has freely given us" (1 Corinthians 2:12).

This ministry of the Holy Spirit is confirmed in another of Paul's petitions. He prays for the Ephesians (and since Ephesians was a "circular letter," we may well assume this represents his prayer for all of God's people): "I keep asking that the God of our Lord Jesus Christ, the glorious Father, may give you the Spirit of wisdom and

revelation, so that you may know him better"
(Ephesians 1:17).

True knowledge of God, then, is not learned
from books (although they may help us); it is not
learned in school or seminary (although they
should encourage it). It is not merely increased
information about God (although such information should stimulate it). No, the knowledge of
God is a *personal* knowledge, the knowledge of a
personal God. It is received by those alone who
seek to know Him in a spirit of dependence upon
Him, and who ask for His Spirit to lead them into
the truth. God's promise is perennially true: "You
will seek me and find me when you seek me with
all your heart" (Jeremiah 29:13). If we *ask*, we will
receive; if we *seek*, we will find; if we *knock*, the
door that opens into the knowledge of God will
swing wide for us.

2. *The knowledge of God involves spiritual wisdom and understanding.* This fundamental truth is
at least assumed in the way Paul prays for the
Colossians. His particular expression, coming
from a man steeped in the Old Testament writ-
ings, is a significant one: "wisdom and understanding" were to be the characteristics of the
Messiah (Isaiah 11:2), as One who would be filled
with the Spirit of God. Indeed, in a lesser sense,
these qualities are the marks of all those who are
anointed by God's Spirit (which is what "messiah" means). So, we find that Daniel, for example—
a man whose whole life breathed the sense of his
knowledge of God—was full of wisdom and
understanding (see Daniel 2:14-30 and 5:12).

But how can we obtain this wisdom and understanding? What instrument, if any, does the Spirit use to produce it? The answer is very simple: He uses the Word of God, which is His living voice.

There is a beautiful, but often overlooked, illustration of this voice of God in one of the poems in Isaiah describing the life, sufferings, and witness of the Servant of the Lord. What is the secret of His life? Here is His testimony:

> The Sovereign LORD has given me an
>   instructed tongue,
> to know the word that sustains the
>   weary.
> He wakens me morning by morning,
> wakens my ear to listen like one
>   being taught.
> The Sovereign LORD has opened my
>   ears,
> and I have not been rebellious. . . .
>   Isaiah 50:4-5

Listening submissively to the voice of God is what brings us the knowledge of God and equips us to teach others and give them spiritual instruction.

Where, then, is that living voice to be heard? In Scripture, and through the patient study and growing understanding of the mind of God as He reveals it there. It is in Scripture that we learn how God views Himself, ourselves, and the world, and what He wants us to know in order to serve Him. Scripture is a working museum of which the Spirit is the Curator, showing us around and explaining the wonders of the mind of the Maker. In this museum we are taken behind the scenes to learn from God Himself. In growing to know God, therefore, there is not a substitute for the discipline of Bible study and Scripture reading and meditation. We cannot bypass the handbook God has given to us and then expect that we can know Him in our own way. The only god we can know in our own way is a god that we make in our own image.

This fact—that we need to persevere in God's Word and abide in Christ's words (John 15:7)—underlines the importance of a third element present in Paul's prayer for the Colossians:

3. *Growth in the knowledge of God requires patience and endurance.* Paul recognizes that those who would grow in the knowledge of God will also need to be "strengthened with all power according to His glorious might," so that they have "great endurance and patience" (Colossians 1:11).

Why should these qualities be so necessary? Because God is a living and personal Lord: He is committed to transforming the lives of His people in order to fit them for the kind of fellowship with Him that knowledge of Him involves. Knowledge, in the sense Paul uses it, means personal acquaintance with God and His ways with us. Sometimes we will discover in our pilgrimage that we do not know or understand what He is doing as He leads us to this knowledge—which means trusting Him even when we cannot understand Him.

James gives us some insight into what this

trust means (see James 5:10-11). He reminds us of the "patience" of Job—or better, his "endurance" (sometimes he was less than patient!). Why did Job need to endure? James' answer is this: although we know what God was doing in Job's life (we have read the last chapters of the book!), *Job did not know* or understand. He needed to learn to endure right to the end, when he finally got a glimpse of the Lord's purposes.

What was God doing in Job's life? Many things—but chiefly, He was bringing Job to a yet deeper knowledge of Himself, so Job could say:

> My ears had heard of you
> > but now my eyes have seen you.
> Therefore I despise myself
> > and repent in dust and ashes.
> > > (Job 42:5-6)

Job had thought he knew God rather well. But he knew that he had been given a knowledge of God of an altogether new dimension.

What would our present age make of the school of discipleship in which Job learned to know God? What is written in capital letters in Job's life interprets the small letters that spell out the same principle in our lives. Those who would know God go through both darkness and light, down into valleys as well as up over hills. The purpose of God is not always immediately evident. To learn to know Him, we must learn to wait for Him (see Habakkuk 2:3). That requires patience and endurance!

4. *The knowledge of God can never be separated from a life of faithfulness.* Paul prays that the Colossians may grow in the knowledge of God because he wants them to live lives worthy of God.

What are the marks of a life that is "worthy" of God? To be "worthy" of something means that there is a correspondence between ourselves and what we are to be "worthy" of. Paul prays that our lives may correspond to God's character.

In practical terms, this correspondence means that the knowledge of God we receive from His Word and learn to appreciate in our walk with Him must be exhibited in the quality of our faithfulness to God and in the integrity of our lifestyle. We are to "make the teaching about God our Savior attractive" (Titus 2:10). There is no such thing as genuine knowledge of God that does not show itself in obedience to His Word and will. The person who wants to know God but who has no heart to *obey* God will never enter the sacred courts where God reveals Himself to the soul of man. God does not give divine knowledge to those who have no desire to glorify Him.

+   +   +

The knowledge of God is our greatest privilege. Yet it is perhaps the Church's greatest need today. It may also be your greatest need just now. You may well profess to enjoy eternal life. But when that life is defined in Jesus' terms rather than your own—knowing the true and living God—how extensive is your experience of eternal life? Is it your boast that you "know the Lord"?

We need to let these questions sink into our hearts and consciences with devastating effect. If we are ever to have knowledge of God that is worthy of the name, we need to be brought low to see our ignorance. If we are ever to learn that knowledge of God that He gives to those who depend on His Spirit, we need to be emptied of our independence.

The following chapters try to unfold the greatness of God, because developing a heart for Him must involve knowing and understanding who He is. But before we go on, we need to turn aside in prayer, to seek the Lord while He may be found, and call upon Him while He is near.

Come, thou Fount of every blessing
Tune my heart to sing thy grace;
Streams of mercy, never ceasing,
Call for songs of loudest praise.
Teach me some melodious sonnet,
Sung by flaming tongues above;
Praise the mount! I'm fixed upon it,
Mount of God's unchanging love.

O to grace how great a debtor
Daily I'm constrained to be;
Let that grace now, like a fetter,
Bind my wand'ring heart to thee.
Prone to wander, Lord, I feel it,
Prone to leave the God I love;
Here's my heart, O take and seal it,
Seal it for thy courts above.

Robert Robinson

2
Three Personed God

Imagine that you are in a sparsely furnished and dimly lit room in the Near East. It is evening, and you are with a group of men, most of them in their early twenties. A special meal is being served.

One man dominates the scene. He is apparently the leader of this group of friends. He also seems to be their teacher, because He is speaking to them with quiet intensity and at some length. He is Jesus of Nazareth. The location is an upper room in Jerusalem; the meal is the Jewish Passover.

You know what Jesus knows—but these young men have only a vague understanding. You know that within twenty-four hours Jesus' body will be hanging, lifeless, on a Roman gibbet outside the walled city. He will have been mocked, scourged, beaten, interrogated, betrayed, denied, humiliated, screamed at, spat upon, nailed to a tree, and lifted up to die. What do you expect to hear now from His lips in these circumstances?

Perhaps you expect an exhortation to faithfulness—and you can find that in the Gospel record of His last hours. You will certainly expect expressions of His love for these men who have left everything to follow Him—and that too you will find in the Passion narratives. But there is a theme running throughout Jesus' teaching in the upper room (recorded in John 13-17) that few of us would expect to find: Central to Jesus' message to His disciples on that last night was His revelation and exposition of the Trinity!

Stunning, isn't it? If it is true. After all, hasn't this doctrine of the Trinity caused problems and even divisions in the history of the Christian Church? Wasn't there virtual war in the early centuries of the Church's life over this doctrine?

True. But this controversy can be interpreted and reacted to in different ways. Either it means we should avoid like the plague even thinking about the Trinity! Or, it means that the very heart of the Christian gospel depends on the Trinity— which explains why the battles were so fierce.

Jesus' teaching in the upper room suggests that the second interpretation is the right one. The amount of time in His sermon on that occasion devoted to the relationships between the Father, the Son, and the Spirit underlines for us how central this teaching must be. It also suggests that if Jesus concentrated on this subject in His darkest hour and at the time of His disciples' greatest need for comfort and encouragement, then the doctrine of the Trinity must have the most practical and important of repercussions.

Just as when good men come to the end of their lives they want to say something of lasting significance to their children, what Jesus said in John 13-17 is intended to bring us into a new and glorious knowledge of God as He really is. That is why this "Book of Glory" (as the last section of John's Gospel is sometimes described) begins with an extraordinary description of Jesus' identity as the Son of God, His humility in washing His disciples' feet, and an acted-out parable describing His descent from glory to the Cross and His return to the right hand of His Father:

> Jesus knew that the time had come for him to leave this world and go to the Father. Having loved his own who were in the world, he now showed them the full extent of his love. . . .
>
> Jesus knew that the Father had put all things under his power, and that he had come from God and was returning to God; so he got up from the meal, took off his outer clothing, and wrapped a towel around his waist. After that, he poured water into a basin and began to wash his disciples' feet, drying them with the towel that was wrapped around him. . . .
>
> When he had finished washing their feet, he put his clothes on and returned to his place. "Do you understand what I have done for you?" he asked them. (John 13:1,3-5,12)

This rite was an act of immense humility. Jesus, the disciples' Lord and Master, had washed their dirty feet. But it was more than a single act—it was also a vivid parable of all that He had done and would do for them. It was a picture of His coming from God, laying aside the expressions of His eternal glory, becoming man, taking the servant's place on the Cross, dying for them, and then returning to His rightful place with His Father.

It is fascinating to place this event side by side with Paul's explanation of what he calls "the mind of Christ" which is found in Philippians 2:5-11:

Being in very nature God, he did not consider equality with God something to be grasped.	Jesus knew that the Father had put all things under his power.
He made himself nothing.	He got up from the meal, took off his outer clothing.
Taking the form of a servant, he humbled himself to the death of the cross.	He wrapped a towel around his waist . . . and began to wash his disciples' feet.
God exalted him to the highest place.	When he had finished washing their feet, he put on his clothes and returned to his place.

At the name of Jesus
every knee should bow
. . . and every tongue
confess that Jesus Christ
is Lord.
       (Philippians 2:5-11)

"You call me 'Teacher'
and 'Lord,' and rightly
so. . . . Now that you
know these things, you
will be blessed if you do
them."
       (John 13:1-17)

In the upper room, Christ's incarnation was presented in microcosm. It was intended to be a visual introduction to teaching that would bring the disciples to a knowledge of God (John 17:3) in a depth they had never before experienced. That is why so much of the teaching that followed Jesus' act of washing set out to explain to them the relations between the Father, the Son, and the Holy Spirit. In many ways, if we are to understand the glory of the Trinity (and not just the "formula" the Church has used to describe the Trinity), it is in the upper room that we must begin.

The Son with His Father and His Spirit

The opening words of John 13, which we have already noted, stress a simple and beautiful fact about Jesus: His home was with His Father. What He did in washing the disciples' feet would have been an act of humility if any one of them had performed it. But the One who actually performed it had "come from God." The disciples confessed this truth before they left the table and went to Gethsemane: "This makes us believe that you came from God" (John 16:30).

John began his Gospel with that truth. The

Lord Jesus is the One who was "in the beginning
. . . with God" and "was God." He is the One
through whom "all things were made." He is the
"one and only Son who came from the Father."
Although He came after John the Baptist, John
confessed that Jesus "was before me" (*not* "is
before me").

The presence of God is where Jesus comes
from and where He belongs. There never was a
time when Jesus did not exist; for He was in the
beginning, with God, and He was God! Later, in
His prayer in John 17, Jesus would make the most
explicit claim to eternal deity to be found anywhere in the Bible, when He asked that He would
return to the glory He enjoyed with His Father
(the glory of God Himself). All this, and perhaps
more, is intended by John when he says in 13:3
that Jesus *knew* that He came from Heaven, from
the presence of the Father.

Perhaps the first chapter of John's Gospel reflects
the words of the personified "Wisdom" in the
Book of Proverbs:

> I was there when he [God] set the heavens in
>   place,
> when he marked out the horizon on the face of
>   the deep,
> when he established the clouds above
> and fixed securely the fountains of the deep,
> when he gave the sea its boundary
> so the waters would not overstep his command,
> and when he marked out the foundations of
>   the earth.

Then I was the craftsman *at his side.*
I was filled with delight day after day,
rejoicing always in his presence. . . .

(Proverbs 8:27-30)

There are several important aspects of Jesus'
relationship with the Father and the Spirit that
emerge in the upper room:

1. *Jesus is conscious of the uniqueness of His
relationship with His Father.* Jesus refers to God as
His Father on more than forty occasions in the
course of His teaching and prayer in John 13-17!
And it is clear that Jesus was not simply the first
one to make a discovery that all men can now
make: the relationship is exclusively between
Jesus and His Father. He and His Father are one.
No one can come to the Father except through
Him (see John 10:30, 14:6, 14:9). To love Jesus is
to love His Father; to obey Him is to obey His
Father. To know Him is to know the Father (John
14:7,21,23).

There is a beautiful passage earlier in John's
Gospel in which Jesus describes His relationship
with God:

"The Son can do nothing by himself; he can do
only what he sees his Father doing, because
whatever the Father does the Son also does. For
the Father loves the Son and shows him all he
does. Yes, to your amazement he will show him
even greater things than these. For just as the
Father raises the dead and gives them life, even
so the Son gives life to whom he is pleased to

give it. Moreover, the Father judges no one, but has entrusted all judgment to the Son, that all may honor the Son just as they honor the Father. He who does not honor the Son does not honor the Father who sent him." (John 5:19-23)

Here is a picture of the unique companionship and friendship which a Jewish father might have with his son, walking with him, teaching him everything he knows. Jesus claims the same kind of relationship to God. How we respond to Him is how we respond to God the Father. They are one—so much one that Jesus will ultimately be the judge of men and nations.

2. *Jesus speaks of His mutual indwelling with the Father.* Even the greatest theologians have never found words to describe what Jesus meant when He said, "I am in the Father and the Father is in me" (John 14:11). As sometimes happens in theological circles, in order to say something about the unfathomable, rather than nothing, a Latin tag has been attached to it: *circumincessio,* or circumincession! This impressive term simply means that the Father and Son "indwell" each other. Here we run up against the mystery of God. And Jesus tells us there is a parallel to it: believers "dwell" in Him and He "dwells" in them.

All that belongs to the Father belongs to Jesus the Son as well (John 16:15). There is complete unity and harmony. The Father loves and trusts His Son; the Son loves and trusts His Father.

3. *Jesus' glory is promoted by His Father.* When you read through the upper-room chapters in John you will notice that at one point in the evening a sense of great relief seems to have come to Jesus. John 13:18-30 records the drama of Judas leaving the company and going out into the night. Jesus had been "troubled in spirit" until that point. But when Judas left, a new theme came to His lips: "When he [Judas] was gone, Jesus said, 'Now is the Son of Man glorified and God is glorified in him. If God is glorified in him, then God will glorify the Son in himself, and will glorify him at once'" (verses 31-32).

Jesus was speaking about His death as the pathway to His resurrection, ascension, and return to His Father in glory. Through His death He would pay the ransom price for sin; in His resurrection He would be vindicated. Through His return He would send His Spirit into the world to bring the nations to faith—indeed, He would be glorified. So He prayed, later (John 17:1-5), that it would be just as God had promised. Nothing could more clearly underscore Jesus' oneness with God. He shared His glory; He brings Him glory; He receives glory from the One who has said, "I will not give my glory to another" (Isaiah 42:8).

4. *Jesus' glory is furthered by the Spirit.* The reason for the sending of the Spirit at Pentecost, Jesus says, is, "He will bring glory to me by taking from what is mine and making it known to you"— that is, the Spirit will take what Jesus, as Son, shares with His Father (since "All that belongs to the Father is mine"; John 16:14-15).

The Day will come, according to Jesus, when His glory will be seen by all (see Matthew 24:30). Here Jesus adds a further dimension to the revelation of His glory. The glory of His deity can be seen *now*, through the ministry of the Spirit. Therefore, we can say with John, "We have seen his glory, the glory of the one and only Son, who came from the Father, full of grace and truth" (John 1:14).

Jesus' glory is made known to us through the Spirit when we come to recognize who Jesus really is, as God's Son and our Savior, as the Creator and Sustainer of all things. This recognition is part of what Paul meant when he said, "'No eye has seen, no ear has heard, no mind has conceived what God has prepared for those who love him'—but God has revealed it to us by his Spirit" (1 Corinthians 2:9,10).

What higher testimony to the deity of Jesus could there be? His Father and the Spirit of God both show His glory to men—the glory He had with His Father before the foundation of the world (John 17:24).

+   +   +

There is another strand of teaching that Jesus weaves into His last sermon: He teaches His disciples about the Holy Spirit as well as about Himself.

The Spirit with the Father and the Son
Often, when the Church has tried to show the deity of the Holy Spirit from Scripture, it has concentrated on passages that speak of His per-

sonal attributes (He "commands," or "forbids," or is capable of being "grieved") and His sharing in the work of God. Jesus takes that further in the upper room. He tells us that the Spirit is "another Counselor"—literally, "another of the same kind," another like Jesus Himself (John 14:16). All that can be said about our Lord, therefore, can also be said about the Spirit.

But perhaps the most striking thing Jesus says here is that the Spirit does what the Father does—His heart is set on glorifying the Son because of His work. So, says Jesus, the Spirit will "bring glory to me by taking from what is mine and making it known to you. All that belongs to the Father is mine. That is why I said the Spirit will take from what is mine and make it known to you" (John 16:14-15).

These words reveal two important truths. First, what belongs to the Father belongs to Jesus. But, second, *the Spirit has the authority and power to show us what belongs to Jesus and the Father*. In domestic terms, the Spirit can use what belongs to the Father and the Son as though He were a co-owner, or partner, in what They possess. And He is!

Earlier in His sermon, Jesus provides some insights that help us to understand this deep and mysterious teaching more fully. In a sense, He removes the obscurity that often surrounds the Holy Spirit—the sense so many Christians have that the Spirit is a kind of "anonymous" member, a "neutral" party in the Trinity. In John 14:15-27, we are told that the Spirit is a Teacher, an Advocate, and a "Homemaker"!

He is a Teacher, because He teaches the Church about the love that flows between the Father and the Son. "On *that* day" (the Day when the Spirit comes) "you will realize that I am in my Father" (John 14:20).

He is a Teacher also because He teaches the Church about Christ's love. "On that day" (the same day!) "you will realize . . . you are in me and I am in you." Only the Spirit of God, who is God Himself, could ever have access to this information and really assure us that it is true.

The Spirit is an Advocate (John 14:16,26; 15:26; 16:13). This word describing the Spirit's ministry is the same word that John later used for Jesus (1 John 2:1). In John's day, as well as our own, an advocate was someone you called to your side to help you. For Jesus' contemporaries, that advocate might simply have been their best friend. I can't think of a better way to describe what Jesus means when He calls the Spirit the Advocate than this: He is "Jesus' best friend," whom Jesus calls alongside Himself to work in our hearts, bringing us to the knowledge of God which is eternal life (John 17:3). According to Scripture, that relationship was true not only in the upper room but also in creation, when the Spirit of God hovered over the waters, bringing order and light from chaos and darkness. It was true when Christ spoke in the men who wrote the Old Testament, who were carried along by the Spirit (2 Peter 1:21). It was true in the Incarnation, and ministry, and death and Resurrection of Jesus—in all of which the Spirit had a role. Who else but the Divine Spirit could stand side by side with the Divine Son?

Most picturesquely of all, *the Spirit of God is the Divine Homemaker.* "You know him [the Spirit]," Jesus says, "for he *lives with you* and will be *in you*" (John 14:17). Put in other words, this truth lies in Jesus' assurance, "I will not leave you as orphans; I will come to you" (John 14:18). Put in yet other words, this truth lies in Jesus' promise, "If anyone loves me, he will obey my teaching. My Father will love him, and we will come to him and make our home with him" (John 14:23).

Apart from God as our Father, we are orphans. But God's own Son has become our Older Brother. He comes through His Spirit, with His Father, to live with us. The Holy Spirit dwells in our lives, making us a suitable dwelling place to receive the Father and the Son! As a consequence, by the Spirit we learn that we are not abandoned and unloved, but rather that we are loved by the Father, by the Son, and lovingly cared for by the Holy Spirit (John 14:21).

In the following chapters, we will examine together what Scripture has to say about the character of God—His holiness, His wisdom, His creating and saving power. We will ask what it means to come to know Him better. But we need to begin here, with the Trinity. It is the profoundest truth of the Bible, and we could be forgiven for thinking that it should be left until the end. But it is not the end; it is the beginning. Before all worlds, God was—Three in One and One in Three—eternal Trinity.

In the upper room on the night of the Passover, Jesus decided that this great mystery of the Trinity was the teaching His disciples most needed to hear. Why was this truth so important? Because Jesus wanted His disciples, and us, to come to know God, in all the riches and fullness of His being. He wanted us to know God in His eternal glory and to recognize how great He is; but He also wanted us to see that the God whose being we cannot comprehend is also the God who is a Father who loves us, a Son who came to die for us, a Spirit who brings us into God's heart and who brings God into our hearts.

On that night in which He was betrayed, Jesus preached the doctrine of the Trinity to His disciples because He knew that in the last analysis, only the people who know their God can stand firm in days of trial (see Daniel 11:32). As you study the biblical teaching on God's character and work, remember that He is not a distant God, but One whose inner being was revealed by Jesus in the most critical hours of His life on earth. And pray that this Three Personed God will reveal Himself more fully to you through Scripture, that you may come to know Him—in the knowledge that is eternal life. Search for this knowledge with all your heart, so you might learn to pray, with John Donne,

> Batter my heart, three personed God; for You
> As yet but knock, breathe, shine, and seek to mend;
> That I may rise, and stand, o'erthrow me, and bend
> Your force, to break, blow, burn, and make me new.
> I, like an usurped town to another due,

Labor to admit You, but oh! to no end;
Reason, Your viceroy in me, me should defend,
But is captived and proves weak or untrue.
Yet dearly I love You, and would be loved fain,
But am betrothed unto Your enemy.
Divorce me, untie, or break that knot again,
Take me to You, imprison me, for I
Except You enthrall me, never shall be free;
Nor ever chaste, except You ravish me.
                    John Donne (1572-1631)

3
Maker of Heaven and Earth

"In the beginning God created the heavens and the earth" (Genesis 1:1). Few words in the Bible are more familiar to us. But that very familiarity has a tendency to dull our sense of the radical nature of these first words of Genesis.

When these words were first written, they presented a challenge to all religions of the world. They made a claim for the God of Israel, the God of the Bible: He alone is God; He alone is the Creator. Ever since, they have challenged philosophies and world views of mankind, and continue to do so today. They affirm, without reservation, that the universe in which we live is not an accident, not the chance result of "nature" or "evolution." It is the handiwork of the living God.

These simple words in Genesis 1:1 have a profound effect on the way we think and live. They teach us that life is not a series of random events, but a miracle that God brought into being. We are not merely the products of a "survival of the fittest" struggle; we are the creatures of a wise, good, and holy God. This world in which we live did not just "happen." It was created with a purpose. We are not alone in the universe, since before we or our forefathers had life and breath, God *was.*

Without this knowledge, the world would be a dark place. But instead it is a theater in which the greatness of its Creator is displayed, and in which we may learn our part as worshiping creatures. God has made the heavens and the earth, things visible and invisible. By contrast, all the gods of the nations (and for that matter, the gods of modern man—Science, Progress, Materialism, Nature, Evolution, so often written with capital letters!) are but dumb idols made by man himself (Psalm 96:5). The unbelieving man, whether he is an agnostic, an atheist, or anything else, ultimately has nothing to make his heart sing. By contrast, the Christian is filled with heavenly praise: He knows that his God is worthy to receive glory and honor and power, for He created all things, and by His will they were created and have their being (Revelation 4:11).

+   +   +

It is often said that the greatest philosophical question is, "Why is there something, and not nothing?" Apart from our conviction that God *is,* and that He is the Lord described in Scripture, there *is* no answer. At best the most distinguished scientist may be able to describe *what* has happened, in order to explain how "something" came to be here. But *why* it should have happened remains unanswered apart from the revelation God gives. As Christians, and students of Scripture, we are not left in any doubt. God made all things *for His own glory,* for "from him and through him and to him are all things. To him be the glory forever! Amen" (Romans 11:36). That is why the Scriptures tell us that "the heavens declare the glory of God" and "the whole earth is full of his glory" (Psalm 19:1; Isaiah 6:3).

Have you ever paused to meditate upon this revelation in Genesis? It can have a stunning effect on our thinking: *We might never have existed.* We might never have had opportunity to think about ourselves, or about the universe, or about God! We are not necessary beings; God has no "need" for our existence. Yet He chose to make this world and to place us in it as His creatures! What a staggering privilege He has given to us, and how unworthy we are (because we have done nothing to deserve our own existence), and how often our ingratitude must grieve Him!

But Scripture wants to expand our minds more to help us see the great privilege of our creation. For while the opening words of the Bible tell us that God has made us, it takes the rest of Scripture to tell us who this God is, what He is like, and what amazing lengths He has gone to in order to bring us to know Him as our great Creator. It is the Three Personed God who has brought us into being. "There is but one God, the Father, from whom all things came and for whom we live; and there is but one Lord, Jesus Christ, through whom all things came and through whom we live" (1 Corinthians 8:6). And we know that the Spirit of God was "hovering over the waters" (Genesis 1:2), participating in the work of creation. God the Father, God the Son, God the Spirit, worked together to bring us and all things into being! The thought is as staggering as it is wonderful.

What, then, are we meant to learn about God and ourselves from the Bible's teaching on creation? That itself is a biblical question, as the writer of Psalm 8 reflected: "What is man . . .?" He was asking not for a scientific answer, but for a theological one. In response, Scripture suggests that the work of creation tells us about the *power of God* and about the *love of God*.

1. *The Power of God.* Man is weak. He is weak by comparison with God, because he is a creature. He is weak by comparison with the universe, because he is so small. He is weak, too, because of his sin. He needs power.

When we turn to God, how do we know that God has the power to help us? Here is the answer: *The God who has the power to create the world in which we live has the power to sustain us in our weakness.*

We sometimes mistakenly think that knowing God the Creator is largely irrelevant; we need to know God as Savior and Keeper. But the biblical emphasis is that the Savior God *is* the Creator

God, and if we are to know how powerful He is as Savior, we must remember that He is the great Creator.

Remember how Isaiah saw God in this way? God's people were to be exiled in Babylon, apparently without hope. Isaiah spoke to them about God's saving grace. He described the Savior God as one who is able to save precisely because He has the power of the Creator:

> Lift your eyes and look to the heavens:
> Who created all these?
> He who brings out the starry host one by one,
>   and calls them each by name.
> Because of his great power and mighty strength,
>   not one of them is missing.
> Do you not know? Have you not heard?
> The LORD is the everlasting God,
>   *the Creator of the ends of the earth.*
>   (Isaiah 40:26,28)

The same pattern of thought occurs in Psalm 121. This psalm pictures a young pilgrim about to make his first trip to Jerusalem for one of the great Old Testament festivals. He is aware of the dangers and difficulties of his journey: He may encounter bandits, landslides, rockfalls. As he lifts up his eyes to the hills in the distance and contemplates his journey, he asks, "Where does my help come from?" Notice the answer he gives: "My help comes from the Lord, *the Maker of heaven and earth*" (Psalm 121:1-2).

There is no greater mistake in understanding

the Bible than to think that this apprehension of
God is an "Old Testament" experience, as though
in the New Testament (by contrast) we know God
as Savior, not Creator. For the New Testament
stresses in a variety of ways how important it is to
know the power of God as Creator if we are to
appreciate His power as Savior.

When Paul was searching for an appropriate
way to describe the power of God in giving life to
dead sinners, he used the language of creation:
"For God, who said, 'Let light shine out of darkness,' made his light shine in our hearts to give us
the light of the knowledge of the glory of God in
the face of Christ" (2 Corinthians 4:6). Later in
the same letter, when he wanted to describe the
power of the new world we have entered into
through Christ, he said, "if anyone is in Christ, he
is a new creation" (2 Corinthians 5:17).

The New Testament does not stop there,
however, in its stress upon God the Creator.
When it wants to emphasize the power of Christ as
Savior, it uses the picture of creation. How do we
know that Christ has the power to save us and keep
us? One answer is because He is the Creator and
Sustainer of all things: "By him all things were
created: things in heaven and on earth, visible and
invisible, whether thrones or powers or rulers or
authorities; all things were created by him and for
him. He is before all things, and in him all things
hold together" (Colossians 1:16-17).

This statement helps us grasp the cosmic
character of our Savior's power when Paul adds:
"And he is the head of the body, the church; he is

the beginning and the firstborn from among the
dead, so that in everything he might have the
supremacy" (Colossians 1:18). In Colossians, Paul
describes the work of Christ as a restoration of *all*
things ("reconciliation" is the word he uses) to
God's original purpose in creation—and all, appro-
priately, through the Creator, the Lord Jesus
Christ Himself!

Knowing God the Creator means knowing
His power. Knowing His power enables us to find
the same comfort and encouragement that Isaiah
gave to his people:

> Why do you say, O Jacob,
>   and complain, O Israel,
> "My way is hidden from the LORD;
>   my cause is disregarded by my God"?
> Do you not know?
>   Have you not heard?
> *The LORD is the everlasting God,*
>   *the Creator of the ends of the earth.*
> He will not grow tired or weary,
>   and his understanding no one can fathom.
> He gives strength to the weary
>   and increases the power of the weak.
> Even youths grow tired and weary,
>   and young men stumble and fall;
> but those who hope in the LORD
>   will renew their strength.
> They will soar on wings like eagles;
>   they will run and not grow weary,
>   they will walk and not be faint.
>   (Isaiah 40:27-31)

The knowledge of God the Creator is the answer to our doubts and our complaints about the way He hides Himself so that we feel neglected. He has made everything, sustains everything, watches over everything. He does not diminish in energy as we do. He is the Creator! He will give us strength and power.

2. *The Love of God.* Creation also shows us God's love and kindness. Students of the Bible are sometimes puzzled by what may seem to be two different accounts of creation in Genesis chapters 1 and 2. But these chapters are complementary to each other.

In the first chapter, the writer describes creation by building up to a climax, culminating in the creation of man. If you read through this chapter slowly, you will notice this pattern in the progression of events: God speaks; a new stage of creation takes place; God rejoices in the goodness of what He has made. Six times this pattern is repeated. But then, quite unexpectedly, a new pattern is introduced in Genesis 1:26. God enters into divine council; He determines to make man—not "according to his kind" (compare verses 11,21,24,25), *but* "in our image, in our likeness." Suddenly we are introduced to an entirely new kind of creature, differently related to God (made in His image), and also differently related to the rest of creation (given dominion over it). Now we realize that man is the apex of God's purposes in creation.

In Genesis 2, the pattern is very different: Man is now introduced not as the apex, but as the center of God's creation. The writer begins with man's creation and then looks at his environment. Obviously, the two chapters go hand-in-hand: As one theologian has written, Genesis 1 shows man as the purpose of creation; Genesis 2 shows him as the beginning of history.

What do we learn about God in these narratives? Fundamentally, that He *lavishes* love and care upon man in every dimension of man's existence. He sets him in a garden, He provides for all his needs, He enters into a relationship of companionship with him. As man's Creator, God is utterly unstinting in the provision He makes for him. This provision is evident in several areas:

First, *God bestows unique dignity on man.* He made everything else but man "after its kind"— that is, according to the purpose and destiny He envisaged for it. But He made man in His own image. Man is patterned on God! He was made to represent God—in created, human form. That is why man has dominion, or rule (Genesis 1:26). He is meant to be to the world what God is to the whole created universe.

This special privilege appears in various ways in Genesis 1 and 2: Man has authority to name the animals; he is able to express rationally the worship of the whole creation; he is the one to whom God speaks His special instructions; he is the one whom God appoints as "caretaker" of the garden He plants in Eden.

Twentieth-century man needs to be reminded at times that *work* is not the result of the Fall. Man was made to work, because the God who made him was a "working God." Man was made to be creative, with his mind and his hands. Work is part of the dignity of his existence (as unemployed Christians often discover when they experience the sense of losing their dignity). When God made man, He ingeniously designed his life and filled it with blessings and privileges. Man is God's special creature, and on him He has bestowed very special privileges and a great and glorious purpose—to serve Him for His glory.

A second aspect of God's creative provision is, *God made man to enjoy fellowship*. God, as Trinity, exists in a fellowship of love. We cannot fully understand this concept, except by saying that there are three Persons in the One God. When we say "God is love," therefore, we know that this declaration is true from eternity. God loves "Himself" in the love that each of His Persons has for the others. He exists both in unity and in fellowship.

When God made man, He made him to experience fellowship too. Of course, man had fellowship with God, but God wanted man to experience fully what it meant to be in His image, by having fellowship with others like himself. It is in that context that the animals were brought to Adam in order to be named. Adam "gave names to all the livestock, the birds of the air and all the beasts of the field" (Genesis 2:20), but none of these animals was suitable to be a companion and helper to Adam. Ultimately, a dog cannot really be "man's best friend." So God created the woman to be a "suitable helper." She was someone like Adam, yet different from him, to stand beside him before God.

We learn two things from this creation of man and woman. One is that friendship and fellowship—with men and women—is part of what we were made for. And what a beautiful gift friendship is! How right it seems to have friends with whom we can "pick up the pieces" even though we may not have seen each other for many months, perhaps even a year or two. I remember having some correspondence with someone whose letterhead bore the words: "How good it is to have such friends about whom one cannot think without elevation!" How true! And it is a gift from God the Creator to enjoy it.

The other thing we learn here is that God has planned marriage. That does not mean that all of us will marry, although Scripture certainly assumes most men and women will (as in fact they do, even in a world that has so largely disregarded God's ways). And whether we are married or not, as Christians we ought to recognize what a priceless gift and blessing from God it is. Marriage has all kinds of purposes: it provides the environment in which children may be born and properly reared. It provides the context in which the sexual instincts can be exercised in a God-intended way. But first and foremost, Genesis teaches us, it provides a very special friendship. In marriage a man and a woman can become the best of friends, knowing each other to such a depth that only God knows them better! This, too, is a gift from the Creator. In His amazing goodness He has given it not just to those who love Him, but to mankind in general. What extraordinary kindness He continues to show as Creator to His creatures, even when they rebel against Him!

God has also shown His love for man in a third provision: *God made man for worship.* On the last day of the creation week, God rested. He therefore "blessed" the seventh day and "made it holy." What does that mean? It means that, for man's benefit, God set aside one day in seven on which man could also rest. The pattern of the Creator in creation, six days of work and a seventh day of rest, was to become the pattern of the creature as he in turn lived a creative life. Here, too, man is the image-bearer of God.

Genesis 2 does not tell us much more about the significance of this seventh day. But as we learn more about it from Scripture we realize that the "rest" involved was not a lazy rest. Rather, it was intended to be a day when the working man could enjoy the Creator as well as the creation. He could devote himself more directly to fellowship with God and the worship of His Name. This "sabbath," or "rest day," was a further special blessing which God gave to man so he would be refreshed and strengthened, encouraged and heartened by contemplating all that God had done and stimulated to worship God in response.

We were made to worship God. We were made to find rest in praising Him. This plan for us is a gift that God in His graciousness and love has given to us as His people. Our "chief end is to glorify God and enjoy Him forever," and we enjoy Him only when we learn what it means to glorify Him, and take (or make) the time to do so.

God did not leave anything undone in making man. He left no need unsupplied. He set man at the summit of His work of creation and blessed him. It is staggering to think that God did not need to do any of that. Has this thought ever really dawned on you? Had the universe never come into existence, His glory would have been complete; had man never been created, His fellowship would have been sublimely joyful. But out of His desire to create creatures He could dignify and bless, He made the universe and set mankind in it. And He entered into fellowship and friendship with man.

+ + +

We no longer live in a garden. Men do not instinctively raise their voices in praise to God. We find work toilsome and often frustrating. Our relationships with others are not all they should be, and often marriage is a source of sorrow rather than joy. What God gave us as the greatest blessings are, for some, the very reverse. The worst is always the perversion and destruction of the best. How very far short we have fallen from God's glory through our sin!

Yet this garden of glory is what God intended us to enjoy. How amazing it is that His Son should enter the wilderness, be tempted by the Devil, know the loneliness and isolation of the Cross, and experience the judgment of God, all in order that Paradise lost might be restored. Because Jesus has done this work, we can now begin to appreciate

God, not only as Savior, but also as Creator. We become what we were always meant to be, and discover the joy of living in our Father's world:

> *Loved with everlasting love,*
> *   Led by grace that love to know,*
> *Spirit, breathing from above,*
> *   Thou hast taught me it is so.*
> *O this full and perfect peace!*
> *   O this transport all divine!*
> *In a love which cannot cease,*
> *   I am His and He is mine.*
>
> *Heaven above is softer blue,*
> *   Earth around is sweeter green;*
> *Something lives in every hue*
> *   Christless eyes have never seen:*
> *Birds with gladder songs o'erflow,*
> *   Flowers with deeper beauties shine,*
> *Since I know, as now I know,*
> *   I am His and He is mine.*
>
> *   George W. Robinson*

4
The Covenant Lord

In my final year of high school we studied Shake-speare's great tragedy *King Lear* in our English Literature class. As I recall, everyone in the small class had already been accepted for study at one of the Scottish universities, so we studied the play in a fairly leisurely and relaxed manner, with plenty of time for thought and discussion. I was fairly confident that I had a good appreciation of the real meaning of the play.

Later that year, during my first term at the university, the senior professor of English Literature gave a series of lectures on *King Lear*. This man was a leading Shakespearean scholar and a brilliant teacher, and I was stunned by the insight and power of his opening lecture. I had learned more about the meaning of *King Lear* in one hour than in all my combined hours of previous study! Now, in a new way, I felt the poignancy and tragedy of the play. The reason was very simple: The professor had taken us to the central motifs, the leading ideas, the "keys" that unlocked all that Shakespeare was wanting to say as he wrote.

The Bible also has some central motifs and key themes. To understand the message of the Author, we need to have an idea of what these motifs are. And to know the Author better, we must learn to think about Him in the way He has revealed Himself to us. Although the Bible reveals God, its Author, many of us miss knowing Him because we do not know how to unlock the Bible's message as it shows us the character of our great God.

One of these key ideas is, *God is a covenant-making and covenant-keeping God.* If you have never thought of Him in these terms, then you have not yet begun to think about Him in the way He wants you to. God's Word describes those covenants, proclaiming Him to be a covenanting God. In a sense, the Bible is the book of His covenant. We even call it that—the Old and the New Covenants (Testaments)!

+   +   +

What is a covenant? The word (*berith* in the Old Testament, *diathēkē* in the New Testament) appears several hundred times in Scripture. It refers to a promise confirmed by an oath of loyalty to the promise. When God makes His covenant with His people, He promises to be their God, and

He binds Himself to that promise. As Hebrews 6:13-18 teaches us, when God made His covenant with Abraham, He staked His own existence on keeping it: He swore by Himself that He would fulfill it, because there was no one and nothing greater by which He could swear His oath!

God's covenant is His marriage bond with His people. He commits Himself to us in unconditional love. Just as in a marriage covenant we do not say, "I promise to love you and cherish you, *but only if* you will . . .," but rather, "I promise to love you and cherish you till death parts us," so it is with God. He does not love us *if* we love Him. He loves us with an unconditional love; *therefore*, we should love Him. The message of the covenant is one of God's totally free grace to His people. Of course, it calls for a response of total commitment! But notice the order: God's covenant love is not the *result* of our commitment; it is the *cause* of it. The pattern is, "I will, therefore you should;" *not* "I will, but only if you will first."

The whole message of the Bible is shaped around God's coming to us in this covenant love. The history of God's purposes of salvation centers on the covenants He made with several individuals, and with their families and posterity. We find God making His covenant with Noah, Abraham, Moses, David, and finally in Jesus Christ. In each of these covenants we discover who God is, and how fully and completely we can trust Him. In fact the message we are meant to hear is this: Down through the centuries God was absolutely faithful to His promises. If He has kept His word all these years, can you not trust Him fully and completely too? *He has proven His trustworthiness and faithfulness.*

God's Covenant with Noah

"Noah" is not a name that many of us choose for our children. But it is a significant name, as Genesis 5:28-29 carefully explains: "When Lamech had lived 182 years, he had a son. He named him Noah and said, 'He will *comfort* us in the labor and painful toil of our hands caused by the ground the Lord has cursed.'" "Noah" means "comfort" or "rest." But notice that his name was chosen in the hopes that he might give the people rest from the labor and toil caused by God's curse on the ground.

What Noah's parents were really hoping was that Noah might be the deliverer God had promised to send in Genesis 3:15 when He cursed the serpent: "I will put enmity between you (the serpent) and the woman, and between *your offspring* and hers: *he* will crush your head, and you will strike his heel." God had turned the blessing of the land into a curse (Genesis 3:17-19). In His mercy, He promised to send a Savior, who would deliver the people from the curse and judgment, and bring them back into the Lord's blessing. It may be that Eve's cry at the birth of Cain was an expression of this same hope: "With the help of the Lord I have brought forth a man" (Genesis 4:1). That hope was tragically unfulfilled—but it did not die. "Noah" gives expression to the longing in the hearts of the people that God's promise—

covenant—would be fulfilled quickly.

A quick fulfillment was not to be; but God did not forget His promise. In later life, it was confirmed to Noah himself. Although divine judgment would fall on the earth, God said to him, "I will establish my covenant with you, and you will enter the ark—you and your sons and your wife and your sons' wives with you" (Genesis 6:18). The word *establish* literally means "to cause to stand." Perhaps there is a hint here that God's covenant would "stand up straight again" after these years in which it seemed to have been hidden from sight. Certainly men had disregarded it and trampled it down. Every inclination of their thoughts had been only evil. God was grieved and determined to bring judgment on mankind. But *He remembered His promise,* and He assured Noah that He would keep the word He had given (in Genesis 3:15). He would be faithful to His promise of judgment. And He would be faithful to His promise of salvation and blessing!

The sign of this covenant was the rainbow. Some Old Testament scholars have suggested that this bow symbolizes a "bow of war": God has thrown His weapon of judgment into the sky, as a reminder of His promise never again to curse the human race in judgment as He did at the flood. That is why from Noah's time until John's vision in Revelation—in which God is seated on a throne of glory encircled by "a rainbow resembling an emerald" (Revelation 4:3)—the rainbow is a sign of God's covenant. But notice what the rainbow communicates: not "Remember God's covenant," but "Remember that *God remembers His covenant*" (Genesis 9:12-17). God is a covenant-*making*, covenant-*remembering*, and covenant-*keeping* God!

God's Covenant with Abraham

The pattern of God's covenant dealings with His people is that they are under His judgment-curse because of their sin; but in His grace, He brings them into His covenant-blessing. We find this pattern in the covenant-promise that God gave to Abraham:

> I will make you into a great nation
> > and I will *bless* you;
> I will make your name great,
> > and you will be a *blessing*.
> I will *bless* those who *bless* you,
> > and whoever *curses* you I will *curse*;
> and all people on earth
> > will be *blessed* through you.
> > > (Genesis 12:2-3)

That was a huge promise. But it was also *incredible*! Abraham had no children. He was seventy-five years old. His wife was sixty-five! And God waited another twenty-five years before He even began to fulfill the promise (Genesis 17:17-18). So when Abraham was taken out by God to view the night sky, he needed all the reassurance he could get to believe the promise: "'Look at the heavens and count the stars—if indeed you can count them.' Then he said to him, 'So shall your offspring be'" (Genesis 15:5).

A strange—and for Abraham, unforgettable—ritual accompanied this promise. Abraham was to kill a heifer, a goat, a ram, a dove, and a pigeon. He cut the animals (not the birds) in pieces, and arranged the dead animals in halves, opposite each other. Then, as the sun set, a deep darkness engulfed the scene, Abraham fell asleep, and later a blazing pot passed between the pieces of animal.

What was God saying? "Let this be my fate, if I do not keep My word and bless you as I have promised. May I be 'cut off' like these creatures." God sealed His covenant by symbolically passing through the middle of them. God was making (literally "cutting") His covenant.

Two elements are important in this symbolism: The first is the terrible darkness. It may symbolize God's judgment. He promises to bless His people even though they are under His judgment because of their sins. The darkness may also symbolize God's hiddenness. As we will see, the promise was not immediately fulfilled. Abraham, and all of God's people, needed to learn to trust God in the darkness. As Isaiah was later to say, "Let him who walks in the dark, who has no light, trust in the name of the Lord and rely on his God" (Isaiah 50:10).

The second important element of this symbolism in the covenant lies in the ritual of the cutting. God was saying, "May I be cut off, like this, if My covenant is not fulfilled." Little did Abraham know how great would be the cost to God of keeping this promise: He would be "cut off from the land of the living; for the transgression of my people he was stricken" (Isaiah 53:8), in order that those who were "cut off" because of their sin, and were under God's curse, might receive the blessing promised to Abraham (Galatians 3:13-14).

God was, and is, faithful to His covenant. But more, He is faithful to His promise even to death—His Son's death—in order to bring blessing and salvation to His people.

God's Covenant with Moses

The story of the Exodus is essentially the outworking of the promise God had given to Abraham. From the time of Joseph, the family of God had gathered in Egypt, waiting for the day when He would fulfill His promise to bring them into their own land (Genesis 15:18). As far as the people could see, God had forgotten His promise and deserted them. They "groaned in their slavery and cried out" (Exodus 2:23). It was a time of deep darkness. It is interesting that when Isaiah describes the return of the people from exile in Babylon in terms of the Exodus, he describes God as "a God who hides himself" (Isaiah 45:15). That is exactly what the Israelites must have felt: "God has hidden Himself; He is not going to keep His promise."

But just the reverse was the case, for God "remembered his covenant with Abraham, with Isaac and with Jacob. So God looked on the Israelites and was concerned about them" (Exodus 2:24-25). He revealed Himself to Moses as the covenant God of Abraham, Isaac, and Jacob (Exodus 3:6). He told Moses *how* He was going to keep His ancient promise.

This was the secret of Moses' life: He held on to the promise of God, not because he immediately recognized how easily it would be fulfilled, *but because it was God who had promised.* He "persevered because he saw him who is invisible" (Hebrews 11:27). But how did he see the invisible God? In His covenant promise!

God's covenant with David

The story of God's covenant with David is narrated in 2 Samuel 7 and Psalm 89. It has all the marks of the covenant with Noah, Abraham, and Moses. But towards the end of his life David reflected on the real significance of this covenant. In doing so, he gives us a glimpse of what it meant (and means) for a child of God to know God as a covenant-keeping Lord:

> The Spirit of the LORD spoke through me;
> > his word was on my tongue.
> The God of Israel spoke,
> > the Rock of Israel said to me:
> "When one rules over men in righteousness,
> > when he rules in the fear of God,
> he is like the light of morning at sunrise
> > on a cloudless morning,
> like the brightness after rain
> > that brings the grass from the earth."
>
> Is not my house right with God?
> > Has he not made with me an *everlasting*
> covenant, *arranged* and *secured* in every part?

> Will he not bring to fruition my salvation
>   and grant me my every desire?
>
> (2 Samuel 23:2-5)

Given David's failures and the confusion in his immediate family circle, this confidence could not have issued from what he saw with his eyes. Rather, his confidence depended on the fact that God had made with him "an everlasting covenant, arranged and secured in every part." Notice these two characteristics that David declared of God's covenant:

1. *It is an everlasting covenant.* When David used this description, he meant that God's promise would be kept in all ages, despite the changes and vicissitudes in his life and in the lives of God's people. God "loved us from the first of time, He loves us to the last." The Old Testament has a word to describe this love: it is *chesed,* loving love, covenant love. The kind of love that Hosea describes when he portrays God's covenant with His people:

> When Israel was a child, I loved him,
>   and out of Egypt I called my son.
> But the more I called Israel,
>   the further they went from me. . . .
> It was I who taught Ephraim to walk,
>   taking them by the arms;
> but they did not realize
>   it was I who healed them.
> I led them with cords of human kindness,
>   with ties of love;

I lifted the yoke from their neck
    and bent down to feed them. . . .

How can I give you up, Ephraim?
    How can I hand you over, Israel?. . .
My heart is changed within me;
    all my compassion is aroused.
I will not carry out my fierce anger,
    nor devastate Ephraim again.
For I am God, and not man—
    the Holy One among you.
                    (Hosea 11:1-4 and 11:8-9)

This is the kind of intimate, family love that
David also sensed his covenant God had toward
him. Considering these loving words, how anyone
could possibly think that the God of the Old Testament is not the God of covenant grace of the
New is something of a mystery! David himself had
wandered from the Lord. He had broken God's
commands. But the Lord had not given him up.
He had kept His covenant promise and shown His
covenant love abundantly to David. So David
wrote in Psalm 89:1-4,

I will sing of the love of the LORD forever. . . .
I will declare that your love stands firm forever,
that you established your faithfulness in heaven
    itself.

You said, "I have made a covenant with my
    chosen one,
I have sworn to David my servant,

I will establish your line forever
and make your throne firm through all
generations."

Everything in the universe might decay and
crumble. But David knew God's covenant promise and His love would never fail!

2. *God's covenant is "well-arranged."* David
declared that God's covenant is perfectly executed
in accordance with God's promise and plan. That
was a statement of *faith,* not a personal opinion.
There were times in David's life when to all
appearances the covenant promise had been ob-
scured, and even seemed to have been destroyed.
No human eye could detect *whether* God was keeping His word, or *how* He would fulfill it. But faith
does not depend on what can be seen! Just as
Abraham grew strong in faith because he trusted
in God's promise instead of reflecting on the age of
his body (Romans 4:20), so David subordinated
the current circumstances of his life to the plan he
knew God would fulfill. There is no other way to
live in fellowship with the covenant Lord.

When I was at the university, I had a friend
who was a medical student from Nigeria. One day
we were talking about hair—his was, typically, a
magnificent "bed" of tightly curled strands. I
commented that he must find it difficult, perhaps
even sore, to untangle it. "On the contrary," he
said, and proceeded to pull out one strand after
another, extending each one, and then letting each
one spring back. I was spellbound, fascinated by
his demonstration. Each hair had its place; there

was not confusion, despite what I had thought. Each one of these thousands of strands of hair had its own place on his head. Everything seemed mixed up, but actually it was in perfect order.

God's covenant is just like that. It may seem impossible to us to tell what He is doing. His promise may seem to be hopelessly entangled in the circumstances of our lives. But He who numbers the hairs on our heads knows each strand of human history, each tiny part of our lives. His purpose is well-organized, and we can trust it. Nothing could be more sure; no pattern could be more perfect than His. We can follow Him through thick and thin with total confidence.

God's New Covenant in Christ

In the days of the prophets, there came a time when the faithful remnant among God's people began to recognize that the covenant had been drastically breached. They had broken the covenant and abandoned God's promise. As they sought comfort in God's presence, and studied His Word, they began to hear Him speak about a "new" covenant. It would center on the Servant of God, who would suffer for the covenant disobedience of His people (see Isaiah 52:13-53:12). The result would be that God would bring people to a true and faithful relationship with Him; His laws would be written on their hearts and His Spirit would move them to new obedience (Jeremiah 31:31-34).

This is the explanation of people like Simeon and Anna (Luke 2:25,38), who were waiting for the redemption and comforting of Israel. In fact much of the background to the *Magnificat* (Luke 1:46-52), the *Benedictus* (Luke 1:68-69), and the *Nunc Dimittis* (Luke 2:29-35) is to be found in God's promise of a new covenant. The faithful remnant in those days believed that God would remember "his holy covenant" (Luke 1:72) just as He had done at the Exodus. A new Exodus would soon take place. That is why when Moses and Elijah appeared with Jesus on the Mount of Transfiguration, they discussed with Him the "Exodus" that He would accomplish in Jerusalem (Luke 9:31, where the Greek word is *exodus*).

The New Testament develops this fulfillment of the covenant further. In the fulfillment of the Exodus in the Old Testament, when the people entered the promised land they renewed the covenant with God. According to Deuteronomy, a strange ritual was conducted. The people were to stand in two groups, one in front of Mount Gerazim and the other in front of Mount Ebal, listening to the reading of God's covenant and law. The blessings and the curses were to be read out (see Deuteronomy 27:15ff), and in response all the people were to say "Amen." We read of this taking place in Joshua 8:30-35. The people bound themselves to God's covenant—both the blessings and the curses—by responding, "Amen."

Why is this strange ceremony so important? Because the New Testament tells us that the Lord Jesus Christ is the "Amen." He is the One who has perfectly said "Amen" to God's law by obeying it. But He is also the One who has said "Amen" to the curse and judgment of God by standing in the place of His people, on Mount Golgotha, and accepting the wrath of God on our sin. He seals the covenant in His own blood. That is what it cost Him to become the "Amen" of God (2 Corinthians 1:20; Revelation 3:14).

Do you see what Christ's death means in this context? God keeps His promise to bless us *through His Son,* but He also keeps His promise to judge and punish men's sins— even when it is *His own Son* who bears those sins.

+ + +

In chapter six we will think more about how God shows His saving love through Christ. But we ought not to move on without clearly fixing in our hearts and minds the lesson we are learning here about our covenant God. *When you look at the Cross, what do you see?* You see God's awesome faithfulness. Nothing—not even the instinct to spare His own Son—will turn Him back from keeping His word. For God promised Abraham that He would keep His word to him, to bring blessing and salvation to mankind through him, even if it meant being "cut off"—as indeed it did.

If, over the centuries, God was planning this terrible climax to His promise, and was utterly faithful to it, can you not trust Him completely? That is the message of the covenant: *God is reliable.* Hold on to that when you too are surrounded by the deepest darkness. If Christ has said "Amen" to God's promises to you, nothing can ever prevent them from being fulfilled!

5
The Ever Present One

Knowledge of God is the foundation stone of all Christian life and service, and all faithful love for God. At least, so Moses discovered. Born into the tribe of Levi, brought up in the palace of Pharaoh, Moses made an early attempt to identify himself with the people of God when he came to the rescue of a Hebrew who was being beaten by an Egyptian. But all his ambitions to be the deliverer of his people came to nothing, and for forty years he was separated from them, tending sheep in the desert.

No doubt Moses felt deserted by God. Moses had hoped he would be the shepherd of Israel, leading them out of their captivity (see Acts 7:25), but instead he had become the shepherd of sheep! He must have had moments— perhaps many of them—when he felt as though God had passed him by. The desert around him symbolized the desert within him. Far from enjoying the sense of God's presence, it is likely he was haunted by a sense of God's absence. His past was marred, his present was insignificant, and his future seemed relatively pointless, given all that God had invested in his life.

Little did Moses realize that he was on the verge of an encounter that would dramatically and permanently change the course of his life. He had led the flock of his father-in-law, Jethro, across the desert to Horeb. *There he met God.* It was a turning point of human history; it was an epoch-making event in God's plan; but it was also the beginning of a new stage in Moses' own life. He could never be the same again.

+   +   +

At Horeb, the Lord appeared to Moses in the burning bush. That strange experience of the burning bush that was never consumed caused Moses to ask two questions which in many ways are the most important questions in the world. Out of the sense of personal inadequacy and weakness he felt in the call of God, Moses asked, *"Lord, who am I?"* Out of a sense of the task to which he was being called, he asked, "Lord, who are you?" (Exodus 3:11 and 13). In these two questions all other questions are summarized.

John Calvin, the reformer, once wrote that the sum of all our wisdom is the knowledge of God and of ourselves. The two can never be separated.

We cannot know ourselves unless we see ourselves as we are in the presence of God. Nor can we come to know God without viewing ourselves in a new light. The presence of God, therefore, does two things: It makes us conscious of who He is, and it makes us aware of who we are in His glorious presence. As Moses stood in the presence of the God who is a consuming fire, but found that he was not consumed, he must have felt as though every last element of superficiality was being stripped from his being. In that context there could be no pretense; nor, in the desert, was there anywhere to hide. He was alone, with God, awed by His presence as the One who called Himself "I am who I am" (Exodus 3:14).

What does it really mean to stand in the presence of God? In the Old Testament, to be "in the presence of God" often translates a Hebrew expression meaning "before the face of God." It conveys the idea of coming face-to-face with Him. More than that, since no man can see God's face and live (as Moses learned—Exodus 33:20), being in the presence of God may carry the sense of standing before One who is able to scrutinize us, who can see all our actions and reactions, in a way that we can never know or understand Him. For God dwells in unapproachable light. What could be more awesome than to stand in the presence of God—and live? There was nothing in the world more awesome that Moses could have done than to stand before the mystery of God's being and the majesty of His glory, and not die. One of our greatest needs in coming to know God in our day is to recover a sense of what it really means to stand in the presence of God.

In their desert encounter, God revealed Himself to Moses in three ways: as the eternal God, as the gracious Savior, and as the ever present Lord.

The Eternal God

When Moses asked God, "What shall I tell the Israelites when they ask me your Name?" he received the enigmatic reply, "Tell them I AM has sent you," because "I am who I am" (see Exodus 3:13-14).

If you were to ask me who I was, and I replied "I am," you might feel annoyed and exasperated. You might well accuse me of trying to hide my identity from you. That is not altogether the case with God. It is true that these strange words teach us that even when God reveals Himself to us, He is never the object of our knowledge of Him, as though we had some kind of "hold" on Him. The reverse is true: We come to know God, never as the object we possess, but as the subject who possesses and knows us. That is why when Paul speaks about us coming to know God, he can add "or rather, are known by God" (Galatians 4:9). So, the God we come to know is not One whose Name can be pronounced "He is," but must always be pronounced "I Am." Coming to know Him means coming to be known and mastered by His knowledge of us. In this sense the Name of God does hide Him from us—if, in asking to know His Name, we are trying to master God rather than be mastered by Him.

Yet the name "I Am" does not, in the last analysis, hide God from us. Rather, it reveals Him to us in a very special way. For what God is saying through His Name is that, while Moses is a man who has had a beginning, has lived through decades of experience, and will one day breathe his last, the same cannot be said about God. God knows neither beginning nor end. He simply *is*—from everlasting to everlasting. Moses came into being, but God *is*—and when we have said that, rather than confuse the truth about Him, we have uttered the profoundest reality of His being. All other things *derive* being—their "is-ness" is secondary. But God did not derive His being from any other—His "is-ness" is underived, original, eternal! He was, and is, and is to come, the eternal "I Am." Rather than conceal His identity, this Name reveals the deepest mystery of His being, and rocks our minds with the discovery that we cannot begin to fathom the mind and life of this eternal God.

This "is-ness" of God's is what theologians call, in technical theological language, the *aseity of God* (from the Latin: *a* = from; *se* = himself—God has His being in an underived way, from Himself). Yet we do not need to be theologians to have a sense of wonder and awe about this truth.

Perhaps, like myself, you used to puzzle about this concept when you were a child. How could God simply be? Where did He come from? Who made Him? How could He exist if He was not brought into being or caused in some mysterious way? I remember being awestruck by such

questions as a boy, realizing that the answers were
beyond me, but that perhaps some day I might
discover them. Now I know that what was a puzzle
to me then is a glorious, divine mystery to me
today. I now realize that the questions that frus-
trated my brain when I was a young boy with no
real faith in the Lord were meant to humble me,
and bring me in awe and reverence to the Rock
that is higher than I am (Psalm 61:2). Try as we
may, God's being defies our understanding. It is
both the mystery of the universe, and its solid
foundation!

But the self-existence of God is the ground of
something else: It is the foundation of all our
worship, and will be the foundation of our praise
for all eternity. That is why, day and night in
Heaven, God's creatures never stop saying: "Holy,
holy, holy is the Lord God Almighty, who was,
and is, and is to come" (Revelation 4:8). No
wonder Moses received a command from "I Am"
to take his sandals off his feet! He was in the
presence of *God*.

Has this truth about God made its intended
impact on your life? Sometimes our thinking
about the Christian gospel is so restricted that we
forget that Paul called it "the gospel of God." We
focus all our attention on one or two favorite doc-
trines. Not so the apostles, whose gospel began
with God and described the glory and majesty of
God. If we are to be whole Christians, we need to
allow the whole of the gospel to make its impact on
our thinking and feeling, our attitudes and every
aspect of our lifestyle.

The fact of God's eternal being makes its impact in different ways. For the unbeliever, it is *absolutely intolerable*. It tells him, "God is God; you are but one of His creatures. Your only joy is to be found in obeying Him, your true fulfillment is to be found in worshiping Him, your only wisdom is to be found in trusting and knowing Him." As Augustine so well said, the heart of the unbeliever will be restless until it finds its rest in God.

These facts are the ultimate threat to the independence, self-centeredness, and sinfulness of the unbelieving man. Of course he says that he has "intellectual difficulties" that make the God of the Christian faith unacceptable to him. But no man or woman ever rejected the gospel on intellectual grounds alone: The ultimate grounds are always moral. The philosopher Nietzsche spoke frankly when he said, "If there is a God, how can I bear not to be God?" That is the real truth about man: he wants to be his own god. He cannot tolerate that Another is God. So he exchanges the truth about God for a lie, and worships and serves something in creation (his house, his car, his family, his sporting interests, money) rather than the Great Creator of all things (Romans 1:21-23).

What Moses (and others of like faith) discovered was that, in bowing before the presence of the Eternal One, a man is stripped of all the facade he presents to the world and to himself. He is constrained to confess, "Lord, I am—for You are from everlasting to everlasting."

The same teaching about the being of God

has a different effect on the Christian: *It brings comfort to the believer.* The psalmists reflect this attitude in a unique way. In Psalm 90, the writer is very conscious of the brevity of life and the apparent insignificance of man's existence. Man is like the new grass that springs up in the morning, but by evening has withered away. In the face of man's feebleness, is there any comfort and encouragement? Yes, there is. The writer says: "Before the mountains were born or you brought forth the earth and the world, from everlasting to everlasting you are God." This is his consolation in a changing world. He can say with the hymn writer "Change and decay in all around I see; O Thou who changest not, abide with me." In effect, that is what he does say, when he confesses at the beginning of the psalm (which is really a summary of the lesson he teaches us in it), "Lord, you have been our dwelling place throughout all generations." In a world of change, of constant fluctuation and apparent chaos, God is always the same!

We find a similar confession in Psalm 46, which pictures the chaos and confusion of the world. Where is sanity and stability to be found? God answers our fearful hearts: "Be still, and know that I am God" (46:10). "I Am" is God! Therefore we can be still, even though "the earth give way and the mountains fall into the heart of the sea, though its waters roar and foam and the mountains quake with their surging. . . . Nations are in uproar, kingdoms fall; he lifts his voice, the earth melts. The Lord Almighty is with us; the God of Jacob is our fortress" (46:2-3 and 6-7).

Because there is no illustration of this in nature—that God *is*, eternal, independent, self-existent—God created an illustration for Moses: A Fire in a Bush which did not depend on the bush for its existence as fire. The Fire burned, independently—like the God it symbolized, whose name is "I Am who I am!"

The Gracious God

Moses was attracted by a fire that did not depend on the bush in which it was burning. But something else about this phenomenon had attracted his attention, which served as a further illustration of the God who spoke to him from within the bush. He said: "I will go over and see this strange sight—*why the bush does not burn up*" (Exodus 3:3). Contrary to all that Moses expected to see, *the fire did not consume the bush.*

Moses did not realize it then, but God was teaching him a lesson about His purposes. He intended to dwell among His people—the God who is a consuming fire (Hebrews 12:29)—and yet His people would be saved, not destroyed. They would learn to say, "Because of the LORD's great love we are not consumed" (Lamentations 3:22).

This lesson on God's purposes was further underlined for Moses in the revelation of God's Name. As most modern versions indicate, the Name can be translated in more than one way. Indeed, it carries more than one significance—not only "I Am," but also, "I will be what I will be." God was also saying to Moses that it would be in the mighty acts of salvation and judgment in the

Exodus that God would show him who He is and what He planned to do. What followed Moses' approach to the bush is very illuminating:

> The LORD said, "I have indeed seen the misery of my people in Egypt. I have heard them crying out because of their slave drivers, and I am concerned about their suffering. So I have come down to rescue them from the hand of the Egyptians and to bring them up out of that land into a good and spacious land, a land flowing with milk and honey—the home of the Canaanites, Hittites, Amorites, Perizzites, Hivites and Jebusites. And now the cry of the Israelites has reached me, and I have seen the way the Egyptians are oppressing them. So now, go. I am sending you to Pharaoh to bring my people the Israelites out of Egypt." (Exodus 3:7-10)

The *verbs* in this passage tell us a great deal. Over and over again, they appear in the first person singular—"I have. . . ." Moses is told not so much what *he* is to do, but what *God* is going to do, in His sovereign power. God plans to take the salvation of His people into His own hands. He will overcome their enemies and set them free. (Later in Exodus, another illustration is used to describe this deliverance: God swoops down like an eagle, snatches His people from Pharaoh, and brings them out of Egypt on outstretched wings—Exodus 19:4. He does what His people cannot do for themselves.)

Notice, however, that there is a certain quality about these verbs in which God describes His activity. He has *seen* His people's misery; He has *heard* their cries; He is *concerned* about their suffering; He has *come down to rescue* them. They all express the concern of the Eternal "I Am" for the condition and needs of His people. They describe His love for them.

Again, we have to look elsewhere in Scripture for what is perhaps the most moving description of the care that "I Am" displayed for His people in the Exodus. It is Ezekiel the prophet who teaches us that the *independence* of God in His eternal self-existence should not be mistaken for His *indifference* to His people's needs. In fact, just the reverse is the case:

> On the day you were born your cord was not cut, nor were you washed with water to make you clean, nor were you rubbed with salt or wrapped in cloth. No one looked on you with pity or had compassion enough to do any of these things for you. Rather, you were thrown out into the open field, for on the day you were born you were despised.
>
> Then I passed by and saw you kicking about in your blood, and as you lay there in your blood I said to you, "Live!" I made you grow like a plant of the field. You grew up and developed and became the most beautiful of jewels. . . .
>
> (Ezekiel 16:4-7)

Yes, Moses would witness God's awesome, saving power. But that power would express the tenderness and exquisite love of a God of infinite grace. God is a consuming fire (see Deuteronomy 4:24; Isaiah 33:14; Hebrews 12:29). He appears as an everlasting burning to dwell in the midst of His people. Yet He does not consume them. He saves them!

The Fire did not depend on the bush; the Fire did not consume the bush; but the Fire was present *in* the bush. Perhaps that points to the third element in this revelation of God's character to Moses: His eternal presence.

The Ever Present Lord

God said to Moses, "I (that is, "I Am") will be with you." But in what sense? The context in which the Exodus is set gives us the answer. The meaning of the Exodus is this: God is remembering His covenant promise to His people (Exodus 2:24 and 6:5). He will keep the promise He gave to Abraham, Isaac, and Jacob. The heart of that promise (as the heart of all God's covenants in Scripture) is, "I will be with you" (Exodus 3:12). God's presence with us is the heart of His promise to us. We can be sure of God, because He has given us His word. And, if God is with us, nothing, ultimately, can be against us!

The longer I have been a Christian the more I have come to see how central this simple truth is. In many ways it is the heart of the gospel— "Immanuel, God with us!" It is also the most basic reality of the Christian's experience.

We must recognize this truth, in contrast to what we are often told. I recall hearing a Christian radio program in which someone obviously facing a major crisis, and possibly great sorrow, asked this question: "What are we to do?" The answer that was given (just a little too easily, I felt) was: "Trust in the God who does impossible things to do the impossible for you." But that is not really a biblical answer. Our consolation does not lie in what God *might* do, although we know He can do anything that accords with His holy will. Our comfort is that *He is with us.* When the mountains in our lives are cast into the seas, here is our encouragement and strength: "The LORD Almighty is with us; the God of Jacob is our fortress" (Psalm 46:7). When we walk through the valley of deep darkness, or the shadow of death, we fear no evil. Why? Because *He is with us.* We do not know whether He will reverse all human expectations and do the impossible. But we have His promise that He will never leave us nor forsake us (Deuteronomy 31:6; Hebrews 13:5). That is why we are able to say with confidence: "The LORD is with me; I will not be afraid. What can man do to me?" (Psalm 118:6-7; Hebrews 13:6).

Have you ever noticed in the story of the burning bush who it is who speaks to Moses and promises to be with him? The Lord who speaks is described in Exodus 3:2 as "The angel of the LORD." It is "The angel of the LORD" who reveals His Name, who promises deliverance, who redeems the people from bondage. Who is the Angel of God, His Messenger, who is Himself the Lord, I Am, and yet One who is sent by the Lord? The rest of Scripture answers our question.

The Angel who appeared to Moses in the bush is the Baby who appeared to men in the manger at Bethlehem. The Angel who spoke to Moses in the desert about the Exodus is the Savior who spoke with Moses on the Mount of Transfiguration about the Exodus, or death to deliver His people (Luke 9:31, where the Greek word *exodus* is actually used). The "I Am" of the burning bush is the same messenger of God who declared: I Am the Bread of Life; I Am the Way, the Truth and the Life, no one can come to the Father except by Me; I Am the Resurrection and the Life. He is the One whom soldiers asked if He was Jesus, and when He replied "I Am," they fell back, staggered by the impact of the momentary revelation of His glorious identity as the Eternal One (John 18:6). Moses saw dimly; we now see clearly. Jesus is God with us. He fulfills the covenant promise of God. In Him we discover the presence of God, Immanuel, God with us.

When we realize this truth of God's presence with us, certain things should follow in our lives, as they did in Moses' life. We should be filled with a new humility, because we have met God. We should be encouraged by a fresh sense of security— we have met God and lived; what else is there to fear? We should be filled with undying gratitude, that God the Lord has worked on our behalf!

Is this the God you know? And is this the way you know Him? When you do, nothing else matters. Or better, everything else begins to fit into its proper place in the service of God. At last there is a song worth singing:

God reveals His presence
Let us now adore Him
And with awe
Appear before Him.

God is in His temple
All within keep silence
Prostrate lie
With deepest reverence.

Him alone
God we own
Him our God and Savior
Praise His Name forever.
                    Gerhard Tersteegen

6
The Savior

Have you ever found yourself returning to a passage in Scripture that, perhaps more than all others, has helped you come to know God better—to appreciate more fully the wonder of His saving grace?

For many of us, Romans 8 provides such a passage. It is the sum and substance of assurance in our faith. It gives us many encouragements but its main concern is to show us the wonder of God's saving grace. That is why Paul makes this statement: "What, then, shall we say in response to this? If God is for us, who can be against us? He who did not spare his own Son, but gave him up for us all—how will he not also, along with him, graciously give us all things?" (Romans 8:31-32).

Paul has waxed eloquent at this point in his letter to the Romans. He is sure that nothing can ultimately stand in the way of God's purposes in our lives. But he can say that as someone who has faced a multitude of obstacles standing in his Christian pathway. He has anything but a "head-in-the-sand" attitude.

In 2 Corinthians 11, the apostle lists some trials he has known: trouble, hardship, persecution, famine, nakedness, danger, sword. This is the man who has been imprisoned, flogged, exposed to death again and again, beaten with thirty-nine lashes no fewer than five times, beaten with Roman rods three times, stoned once, shipwrecked three times, and in the open sea on one occasion for a night and a day. He has often gone without sleep, been hungry and thirsty, cold and naked! When he says that nothing can separate us from the love of Christ, he knows exactly what he is talking about.

Imagine, for a moment, that you are a member of the church at Antioch. The Apostle Paul is a member of the congregation. You became a Christian after he was sent out by the church; you do not know him personally. But now Paul has come back and given his report. You are stunned by what you hear, but your enduring impression of him really comes from something you saw at the church picnic. One of the children in the fellowship asked Paul to come in swimming. Paul was glad to, and slipped off his outer garment. You had never read the letter he wrote to the Galatians, but as he made his way, hand-in-hand with the child, into the water, you read one of its verses on his back: "I bear on my body the marks of Jesus" (Galatians 6:17). Bruises, scabs, poorly healed lacerations—yes, he knew what he was talking about. No wonder you wanted to ask him: "Paul, what kept you going? What was it about God's saving grace that helped you to persevere?"

I think Paul's answer would have been something like this: "God did not spare His Son, but delivered Him up for me. That fact assures me that there is nothing God will withhold from me, if it is for my blessing. It also gives me confidence that God will use every event in my life to bring blessing to me or others. God would not have gone to the lengths He has to save me, if He did not mean to keep me."

In fact, in Romans 8:32, Paul recounts three evidences of God's grace and salvation: "He who *did not spare his own Son,* but *gave him up for us all*—how will he not also, along with him, *graciously give us all things*?" Each of these three tells us something about Jesus Christ.

+ + +

1. *Jesus Christ was not spared by His Father.* Whenever Paul was tempted to think, "God might have spared me that," this truth was what came to his mind: God had not spared Jesus! God did not single out Jesus to give Him special protection from the harsh experiences of life. Indeed, "God did not spare Him" might be putting things as mildly as possible. For from the cradle to the grave, Jesus was certainly not spared!

Think of His early life: Born in a stable, miles away from home; carried by His parents to Egypt for a couple of years; brought up in Nazareth, where perhaps His earthly father Joseph died while Jesus was in His teens or twenties. Then He knew hunger and poverty during His ministry; experienced the grief of misunderstanding and rejection, as well as the sorrows of bereavement; suffered the abuse of others; was eventually betrayed by one of His own disciples and then hours before His death, denied by one of His closest friends; He was beaten, spat upon, and ultimately exposed to public shame and crucified. Jesus was not spared at any time during His life.

But Paul saw something more than human sufferings in this drama of the Messiah's life. He saw something almost *unnatural* about it, which haunted him until it eventually became the source of great comfort and joy to him. He was familiar with God's revelation of Himself as the Father of His people: "I will spare them" God had said through Malachi, "just as in compassion a man spares his son who serves him" (Malachi 3:17). Jesus had served His Father, as a son should serve a father. But contrary to all that is natural, His Father did not spare Him.

Yet Jesus deserved to be spared. He did not deserve to experience the cruelty and malice of men in this world. He did not deserve to be poor, or hungry, or to feel His heart breaking as He stood before the effects of sin in man's life. If only we could see ourselves in the light of God's holiness, we would never defiantly ask, "What did I do to deserve this?" We would know that before God's righteous judgment we deserve nothing good. But Jesus could quite righteously have asked, "What did I do to deserve this?" In a sense that was the meaning of His cry of dereliction on the Cross: "My God, why have *you* forsaken me?" Why had He not been spared? In the horror of His loss of His sense of communion with God, nothing seemed to make sense. There, on the Cross, it must have seemed as though right had become wrong; good, evil; God's righteousness, terrible judgment and condemnation of an innocent man.

Yes, Jesus deserved to be spared. Think of what He had accomplished in His short ministry: He had preached about a Father He knew and loved, and who knew and loved Him. He had introduced a whole generation of men and women to this Father in Heaven. He had healed the sick, given sight to the blind, even on occasion brought men back to life. His words were glorious, His life impeccable, His whole being perfect before both men and God. Everything about Him seemed to point to the conclusion, here is One who deserves to be spared.

But Paul tells us Jesus was not spared. And in saying that, he is simply summarizing the teaching of the Gospels. Yet almost certainly Paul knew something more than just the fact that Jesus was not spared, because he was familiar with at least two of the authors of the Gospels, Mark and Luke. *Paul knew Jesus had prayed that, if it were possible, He might be spared.* In the Garden of Gethsemane, on the night before He was crucified, Jesus had

cried to God, apparently in terrible agony, "*Father,
if it is possible, let this cup* [the sufferings of the
Cross] *pass from me.*" On the Cross He later
cried, "My *God . . .*" but in the Garden, His
appeal was that of a son to a father. What father
could possibly fail to grant his child's cry? *But
Jesus was not spared,* although three times He
asked that being spared might be His Father's
will.

Jesus was right to ask to be spared. He would
have been less than a true man if He had been able
to contemplate the dereliction of the Cross without such a desire. But His right and holy desire
was not to be fulfilled.

Both the Gospel writers and Paul seem to
have realized that Jesus was fulfilling a picture
that had first appeared in the life of Abraham in
Genesis 22, when God had told him to take his son
Isaac (the son whom he loved) and sacrifice him on
Mount Moriah. Perhaps it is to that event that
God was drawing attention at the Baptism and
Transfiguration of Jesus when He said, "This is
the Son whom I love." The Father was virtually
saying, "I am now in the position that Abraham
was in—you must wait to see whether my Son will
be spared or not."

Paul certainly has this Old Testament story in
mind when he writes in Romans 8:32. For the
vocabulary he uses is taken directly from the Sep-
tuagint (Greek) version of the Old Testament he
used. Genesis 22:17 lies directly behind Romans
8:32. Abraham was willing not to spare his own
son, but God commanded him to be spared. By

contrast, God's own Son, the Son He loved, was
not spared.

That is the greatest mystery in the universe.
But Paul puts the message of the gospel like this
for one obvious reason. If what he says is right, we
can draw only two possible conclusions: Either
God is utterly arbitrary and whimsical, impossible
to understand and unworthy of trust; or (as Paul
was convinced) God was doing something in the
death of Jesus Christ, His Son, that is breathtak-
ing in its significance.

+   +   +

2. *Jesus Christ was given up for sinners.* It is
deeply moving to think about the Son of God not
being spared. But in one sense that is just the
surface of what Paul wants to say in Romans 8. It
describes the experience of Jesus in negative
terms. Now Paul fills that with significance when
he says that Jesus was "given up," or handed over,
to the death of the Cross. What does he mean?

The word Paul uses here is almost a technical
term, and it is used as such in the New Testament,
in connection with the death of Jesus. It appears
especially in Matthew's account of the Passion:

> "We are going up to Jerusalem, and the Son of
> Man will be betrayed to the chief priests and the
> teachers of the law. They will condemn him to
> death and will *turn him over* to the Gentiles to
> be mocked and flogged and crucified. . . ."
>   Then one of the Twelve—the one called
> Judas Iscariot—went to the chief priests and

asked, "What are you willing to give me if I *hand him over to you?*" . . .

Early in the morning, all the chief priests and the elders of the people came to the decision to put Jesus to death. They bound him, led him away and *handed him over* to Pilate, the governor. . . .

When the crowd had gathered, Pilate asked them, "Which one do you want me to release to you: Barabbas, or Jesus who is called Christ?" For he knew it was out of envy that *they had handed Jesus over to him.* . . .

"Which one do you want me to release to you?" asked the governor.

"Barabbas," they answered.

"What shall I do, then, with Jesus who is called Christ?" Pilate asked. They all answered, "Crucify him!". . .

Then he released Barabbas to them. But he had Jesus flogged, and *handed him over to be crucified.* (Matthew 20:18-19; 26:14-15; 27:1-2, 17-18,21-22,26)

What is the meaning of the repeated use of this expression in the Gospels? The New Testament suggests that it signifies three central things about the way in which Christ's death brings salvation.

First, it signifies that *Christ's death was judicial.* His death is not pictured as a tragedy anywhere in Scripture. Rather it is seen as a legal process in which Christ was arrested, arraigned, tried, and eventually condemned to death. We even know the charges that were brought against Him: blasphemy and treason. He was accused of blasphemy, because in claiming to be the Son of God He made Himself equal with God. He was accused of treason because, in claiming to be a King, He rebelled against the authority of Rome and of Caesar. He was accused by Jew and Gentile, arrested by the Temple guard, and crucified by Roman soldiers.

Yet the same passion narratives that describe the charges brought against Jesus tell us that no one was able to confirm them. In fact, in decision after decision, Jesus was found innocent. We are perhaps so familiar with the story that we often miss the absurdity and contradiction in what took place. But someone sensitively reading the Gospel record for the first time would be constrained to cry out in protest, "Stop! Don't you see you're contradicting yourselves, Jews and Romans? You are rushing a man to His death when you cannot prove Him to be guilty. You have evidence of His perfect innocence before you, but you will not listen to it! Stop!" This is the contradiction inherent in the Passion: Jesus is innocent. He is declared to be innocent several times (see Luke 23). Yet Jesus is condemned and executed. Why?

Our answer lies in a second central meaning of the expression "handed over": *Christ's death was divinely ordained.* As we trace this term "handed over" through the Gospels, we find that Judas "handed over" Jesus—so he played a role in the crucifixion. We find that the priests "handed over" Jesus, so they shared in the responsibility. We read that Pilate "handed over" Jesus. Various individuals and groups ushered Jesus along to the

Cross. The early church saw these events as the fulfillment of the second Psalm: "'the rulers gather together against the Lord and against his Anointed One.' Indeed Herod and Pontius Pilate met together with the Gentiles and the people of Israel in this city to conspire against your holy servant Jesus, whom you anointed" (Acts 4:26-27).

But another, higher hand appears in the crucifixion of Jesus. Paul says that God the Father "handed him over"! This is not an isolated statement—or some kind of Pauline aberration. Look again at Peter's and John's prayer in Acts 4. After they listed the conspirators in Jesus' crucifixion, they added, "They did what your power and will had decided beforehand should happen" (Acts 4:28). Earlier, on the day of Pentecost, Peter had said directly to the Jews in Jerusalem, with an understanding little short of staggering: "This man was *handed over* to you by God's set purpose and foreknowledge; and you, with the help of wicked men, put him to death by nailing him to the cross" (Acts 2:23).

It was the Father's hand that lay behind all that had taken place in Jesus' death on the Cross. We will never really appreciate what happened on the Cross unless we understand this fact. All the central passages in Scripture that illumine the meaning of Christ's death allude to it. When Jesus explained to His disciples in Mark 14:27 the significance of what would happen to Him, He quoted from God's words in Zechariah—"Awake, O sword, *against* my shepherd, against the man who is close to me! . . . Strike the shepherd, and the

sheep will be scattered . . ." (Zechariah 13:7).
Paul spoke of Christ coming under the curse of
God (Galatians 3:13). He daringly said that God
had made Jesus to be sin (2 Corinthians 5:21)! All
this had been foreseen in Isaiah's prophecy of the
Suffering Servant: "It was the LORD's will to crush
him and cause him to suffer" (Isaiah 53:10).

How can this be, that God would put His own
Son to death? We need to take one final step in
order to understand, and it lies in a third meaning
of the term "handed over." It completes the significance of the purpose behind the plan of the
Cross: *Christ's death was substitutionary.* How
could the Innocent One have righteously been
sent to His death by a Holy Father? There is only
one answer, according to Scripture. Paul supplies
it in Romans 8:32—the Father gave up His Son
"for us all." In His condemnation and death,
Jesus was taking our place. That is why the
charges brought against Him were *blasphemy* and
treason, for these are the very charges we face
before the judgment seat of God. We have made
ourselves into gods, and thus blasphemed His holy
Name; we have rebelled against His rightful rule
over our lives, and we are guilty of high treason
against His gracious majesty.

This is why those same passages that tell us it
was ultimately the hand and purpose of God that
brought Jesus to the Cross also tell us that He died
for us. He was made sin *for us,* although He had no
personal sin. He was made a curse *for us.* He was
pierced *for our transgressions,* crushed *for our iniq-
uities,* punished *for our peace,* wounded *for our*

healing: "We all, like sheep, have gone astray, each of us has turned to his own way; and the Lord has laid on him the iniquity of us all" (Isaiah 53:5-6).

Jesus made what the reformers used to call "the wonderful exchange." He took what was ours, so we might receive what is His. He took our guilt and its punishment; we receive, by faith in Him, His right relationship with God and all the blessings of belonging to the family of God. No wonder Jesus cried out in desolation on the Cross, "My God, why have you forsaken me?" Here is the biblical answer to that question: *He was forsaken in order that we might not be.* This is what we mean when we sing, "In my place, condemned, He stood, and sealed my pardon with His blood. Hallelujah! What a Savior!"

Christ was not spared by His Father. He was "handed over" for us as sinners. These are the first two evidences of God's grace and salvation that Paul gives us in Romans 8:32. But Paul goes further. His statement, "He who did not spare his own Son, but gave him up for us all" is really a description of God intended to explain to us *what God our Savior is like.* We can draw the conclusion Paul wants us to, namely: since this is so, "how will he not also, along with him, graciously give us all things?" All of Paul's concern in stating the meaning of the saving death of Christ has had one purpose in view: to tell us what God is like, so that we will trust Him implicitly.

+   +   +

3. *Jesus Christ is completely trustworthy.* Since

God has given us everything He has, in Christ, how can we ever doubt Him? No matter what the circumstance, we can use this argument: If the Father has given His own dear Son to the darkness and death of Calvary, it is utterly unthinkable that He would *now* send anything in my life, or do anything through my life, that was not for His glory and my eternal blessing. That is why, even when everything might have seemed to be against him, Paul was able to say in Romans 8 that God worked everything together for his good; and that nothing and nobody could ultimately be against him if God was for him. The reason he knew beyond a shadow of a doubt that God was for him was to be found in Christ and what He had done.

Paul's logic is irrefutable. This is the kind of God our saving Father is. Yet how few of us allow our hearts to be molded by this knowledge of Him. One would almost think we preferred to believe that God was against us rather than for us! When we truly belong to Christ, that thought is a lie of the Devil's making. It is the kind of lie he whispered to Eve in the Garden of Eden: "Has God given you this magnificent environment, and then restricted you so that you can't eat from any of the trees in the garden?" (Genesis 3:1). It is the attitude of the older brother in Jesus' parable, who has never entered into a *confident* relationship with his father, but instead sees himself in these terms: "All these years I've been slaving for you" (Luke 15:29). It is the suspicion of the servant who said to his master, "I knew that you are a hard man. . . . So I was afraid . . ." (Matthew 25:24).

Of course this wrong view of God involves bad theology; but it is not by any means an academic matter. It is one of the most central, practical issues in the Christian life. How you view God determines the quality and style of your Christian experience. Many Christians spend much of their lives paralyzed because, although they have trusted Christ as Savior, they have never really seen what His sacrifice teaches us about the character of God. He gave His Son; He sent His Son; He "handed over" His Son because He loves us. He thereby proves His grace.

Do you know this God, in this way? It is possible to have "a heart for God" and yet miss the benediction of His grace, eventually becoming turned in upon your own commitment and zeal, failing to grow more and more into the likeness of Christ. Some "committed Christians" seem to be little like Jesus, often because they do not know what Jesus shows—the sheer depth of a Father's love never more powerful than at the very moment the Father was handing over His Son to be crucified: "The reason my Father loves me is that I lay down my life" (John 10:17).

Have you entered into this relationship of love and trust? Is your heart set on the Father who did not spare His Son for you, but graciously "handed over" Jesus to the Cross, for your sake? If this God is for you, who can be against you?

7
God Only Wise

Unless you become familiar with the wisdom of God, you cannot make much real progress in the Christian life. True stability over an extended period of discipleship will often depend on trusting that God is wise in everything He does and in all His dealings with His children.

The Bible is full of wisdom. Indeed, there are books in the Bible known collectively as "the wisdom literature." They express the idea of wisdom (in God or man) in a rich and varied vocabulary. Wisdom involves training (including correction and instruction); it includes insight and understanding; it involves practical skill and sensitivity, shrewdness and discretion, knowledge and right learning. The wise man is the one who sees his goal, recognizes the best ways to achieve that goal, and then implements those ways. The wisdom of God is similar: God puts His glorious purposes into effect in order to demonstrate His perfect knowledge, sovereign power, and infinite grace. God's wisdom is evident as He takes the raw, fallen materials of this world and its history to weave a garment of praise and glory for His Name.

It is fascinating to notice that in the circular letter Paul wrote to some of the early churches, including Ephesians (the copy that has come down to us), the wisdom of God is one of the minor themes. Paul tells us that the wisdom of God lies behind the planning of the gospel: He has lavished grace upon us "with all wisdom and understanding" (Ephesians 1:8). For men, "wisdom" often involves caution and frugality. But with God and His expressions of love, wisdom dictates that grace should be "lavished on us"!

The ultimate consequence of this expression of God's wisdom appears in the lifestyle of the Church. We learn wisdom from God, and are urged to "Be very careful, then, how you live—not as unwise, but as wise" (Ephesians 5:15). The child of God is urged to become like his Father.

There is a third place in Ephesians where Paul speaks of the divine wisdom, however, and it is the most fascinating of all. In chapter 3 he speaks of the manifestation of God's wisdom through the gospel. Paul describes his own special ministry in terms of a purpose God has had from all eternity, but which has been hidden throughout the previous ages and is only now (particularly through Paul's ministry) being made known. This "mystery" (the New Testament's word for a secret that has now been made public by divine revelation) is the bringing together of Jews and Gentiles into one fellowship. In this way, "His [God's] intent was that now, through the church, the manifold wisdom of God should be made known to the rulers and authorities in the heavenly realms, according to his eternal purpose which he accomplished in Christ Jesus our Lord" (Ephesians 3:10-11).

This is a staggering statement, and we need to pause to reflect on what it says. Paul speaks about the *variety of God's wisdom:* it is manifold. The word he uses means "multi-colored"! God's wisdom is like the rainbow, in symmetry, beauty, and variety. He does not paint scenes merely in black and white, but uses a riot of color from the heavenly palette in order to show the wonder of His wise dealings with His people.

Paul also speaks about the *audience to which God displays His wisdom.* What he says is even more surprising: God shows His wisdom not only for the world to see, but also "to the rulers and authorities in the heavenly realms." He gives a cosmic demonstration of His perfect purposes.

But the most interesting aspect of all is *the sphere in which God makes known His wisdom.* Has that ever jumped out of the page at you as you have read Ephesians 3:13? It is important. Because if you are to trust in God's wisdom, where are you to find proof of it? When you look at the world, or the circumstances of your own life and the lives of others, do you not sometimes doubt whether God is really wise, and don't you wonder if there is anywhere that God demonstrates His wisdom beyond dispute?

William Cowper (who knew a great deal about doubting God's wisdom in his deep personal affliction of mind) saw the problem clearly when he made use of the words of Psalm 77:19 in one of his hymns: "God moves in a mysterious way, His wonders to perform; He plants His footsteps in the sea, and rides upon the storm." Our problem is that we cannot see footsteps in the sea! And when God rides on the storm, He is hidden from us by the storm itself. We are sometimes left wondering just what His plan is. We need somewhere that we can point to and say, "I see His wisdom clearly displayed here—so, even though I do not understand what He is doing in my life, I *know* He is perfectly wise, and is working in these circumstances, too, to bring about His perfect will."

Paul says that God's wisdom has been, and is being, clearly displayed *in the Church*. The Church is a theater in which God portrays the drama of His wisdom so clearly that the rulers and authorities in the heavenly realms cannot mistake it! The Church, he says, is like a microscope. As we see God bringing it into being we recognize His wisdom. What we cannot discern with the naked eye in our own lives, we can see, living and active, in the Church—the wisdom of God!

How is this so? God's multi-colored wisdom is manifested in three different ways in the

Church—in its foundation, its membership, and its sufferings.

+   +   +

First, *The wisdom of God is displayed in the foundation of the Church, in the work of Jesus Christ.* Paul declares in Ephesians 3:11 that God's wisdom is made known "according to his eternal purpose which he accomplished in Christ Jesus our Lord." What Christ has done for us demonstrates God's wisdom. I believe this was one of the things that haunted Saul of Tarsus until he submitted to Christ and was brought into the Kingdom of God. How could Christians claim that the Wisdom of God incarnate was crucified? The idea was utterly incredible to him.

Those earlier struggles in his own mind are probably reflected in what Paul wrote in 1 Corinthians 1:18-2:16. The message of the Cross is not one of wisdom but of folly to an unbeliever, he wrote. What could be more foolish than to believe in salvation through the death of "Wisdom" and the crucifixion of "the Prince of Life"? But Paul later came to see that God's "foolishness" is *wiser* than man's "wisdom," just as God's "weakness" (in the death of Christ) is *stronger* than man's "strength." The paradox (and genius!) of the gospel for Paul was that when the world in its "wisdom" did not know God, God made Himself known through the "foolishness" of the message of the Cross! What had earlier simply angered Saul of Tarsus ("How dare God save men through the humiliation of the Cross!") now filled Paul the

Apostle with unrestrained admiration.

But how does Christ's death on the Cross demonstrate God's wisdom? Simply this: Through the Cross, our sin is judged, yet sinful men and women are forgiven precisely because God has judged that sin in Jesus Christ instead of in us. God has done what seemed morally impossible in a way that demonstrates rather than denies His holiness and justice. That is why the Cross is the "trysting place, where Heaven's love and Heaven's justice meet." The Cross is the expression of God's loving genius. There is something Godlike in the wisdom it displays!

Sometimes scholars have discussed the question of whether the "rulers and authorities" to whom the wisdom of God is displayed in Christ are good or evil. Are they the angels of God, or the Devil and his army? Perhaps both were in Paul's mind.

Imagine, for a moment, the reaction of Hell to the death of Christ. Jesus was bound with the bands of death. What celebration and joy! God was defeated! Vengeance was the Devil's. But they reckoned without the wisdom of God. For Christ could not be held down by the bands of death. In fact through death He was paralyzing the one who had the power of death, and He was setting His people free (Hebrews 2:14-15). What seemed to be defeat was actually victory. The Resurrection morning was Hell's gloomiest day. Satan saw the wisdom of God and tasted defeat.

Think also of the angels in Heaven. Peter tells us they long to look into what Christ did (1 Peter

1:12). Did they hold their breath as Jesus breathed His last, wondering how God's wisdom would be displayed in such apparent tragedy? Did they ask if sinners could possibly be worth such expense to God when He did not spare the angels who had sinned? Imagine their admiration at the resurrection victory of Christ their Prince! No wonder the ancient Church thought of Jesus' ascension in terms of the picture of Psalm 24—the King of Glory returning from His victories in battle, demanding entrance to the City of God: "Lift up your heads, O you gates; be lifted up, you ancient doors, that the King of Glory may come in. Who is this King of Glory? The Lord strong and mighty, the Lord mighty in battle. . . . The Lord Almighty— he is the King of Glory" (Psalm 24:7-8,10). Well might they sing with Paul: "Oh, the depth of the riches of the wisdom and knowledge of God! How unsearchable his judgments, and his paths beyond tracing out!" (Romans 11:33).

But why is this wisdom seen in the Church, or through the Church? Because the life of the Church flows from its foundation in the work of Christ. The Church exists only because of what He has done. At its heart lies a display of divine wisdom greater than any other. And if I belong to the Church, it is only because of the way in which God's wisdom has been displayed in Jesus Christ. The Church is dependent upon Jesus Christ, in whom alone are displayed all the treasures of God's wisdom and knowledge (Colossians 2:3). The Church serves as the microscope that enables me to see a wisdom invisible to the naked eye.

Second, *The wisdom of God is displayed in the membership of the Church, in the fellowship of Jew and Gentile.* This truth is the chief focus of Paul's teaching in Ephesians 3. Paul had realized that part of the meaning of his own life (and the wisdom of God towards him) lay in his being the means through which the "mystery" of Christ would be revealed, "which was not made known to men in other generations as it has now been revealed by the Spirit to God's holy apostles and prophets" (Ephesians 3:5). What *is* this mystery? It is that "through the gospel the Gentiles are heirs together with Israel, members together of one body, and sharers together in the promise in Christ Jesus" (Ephesians 3:6).

This union of Gentile and Jew in Christ was a major element in the ministry to which Paul had been called on the Damascus Road. The Lord had told Ananias that Paul was His chosen instrument to bring the gospel to both Gentile and Jew (Acts 9:15).

Perhaps in the 1980s we are again catching a sense of the wonder of this convergence in Christ, as young people from Jewish backgrounds world-wide seem to be turning to faith in Jesus as the promised Messiah. But many of us have become so accustomed to the Gentile character of the Church that we overlook the fact that we have heard and responded to the gospel *as Gentiles,* and have been grafted into the olive tree which God planted in His ancient people (Romans 11:17-24).

Paul tells us that we should be constantly amazed when we remember that the Gentile

Church has its roots in a Jewish world. Who could have anticipated what God did? It was a secret, a mystery that God kept largely to Himself before the coming of Christ.

We can look at the implications of this mystery in two ways. On one hand, the wisdom of God in Jesus Christ *brings Jew and Gentile together.* Paul had expounded this fact in Ephesians 2. Jewish believers and Gentile believers are brothers in Christ, sharing the covenants and promises, members of the same family, citizens of the Kingdom of God. The wall dividing us has been broken down! But how? Amazingly (for Paul), through the humiliation and death of the Jewish Messiah!

But there is a second implication in what Paul says about this mystery: The bringing together of Gentile with Jew involves the bringing together of *Gentile and Gentile.* In Christ, Paul says, "there is no Greek or Jew, circumcised or uncircumcised, barbarian, Scythian, slave or free, but Christ is all, and is in all" (Colossians 3:11). The Church is the imperfect, visible form of God's heavenly Kingdom. In it the barriers we have erected in our sin are broken down, because Christ dwells in each member of His Church. The same Christ dwells in you who dwells in me! How then can we erect barriers between each other? Further, in the Church Jesus Christ is *all* to all in the fellowship. We all trust Him, love Him, worship Him, and want to serve Him. One common goal dominates everything we do—to please Christ. When that happens, everything else is of secondary importance—wealth, background, education, class, race,

nationality, all are given a secondary place. Out of
the chaos of the differences among men, God
makes a glorious tapestry for His glory, a multi-
colored landscape of His wisdom.

Isn't this one of the great joys of belonging to
a living Christian church? To be able to look
around during church gatherings, and marvel at
the way in which God has brought us by different
paths to the same Christ—some rich, some poor,
some wise, some simple, some with one accent,
some with another, yet all members of the same
family. Not only so, but as we look around, we see
some who have suffered, some who have shown
great faith, some who have been restored from
their backsliding, some who have great gifts, some
who have shown us Christ's love in a special way.
It can be said of God's wisdom, as it is written of
Sir Christopher Wren in St. Paul's Cathedral,
London: "If you are looking for his monument,
look around you!" The Church, as a living fellowship, is the multi-colored monument that God has
erected of His wisdom. There we can see—if only
we will look—how marvelous His wisdom is. We
can see in what He has done on the larger canvas of
human history that all He does is perfectly wise.
We can see, too, on the smaller canvas of the lives
of our brothers and sisters, that He does everything wisely, and works everything together for
good for those who love Him and have been called
into His purpose (Romans 8:28).

+   +   +

Third, *The wisdom of God is displayed in the*

suffering of the Church, in the experiences of the servants of God. At the conclusion of his teaching in this section of Ephesians 3, Paul says: "I ask you, *therefore,* not to be discouraged because of my sufferings for you, which are your glory" (3:13). The word "therefore" is a rather important one in Paul's writing. It *joins together* the teaching he has been giving with the practical application and conclusion to which it gives rise. That is why we sometimes say to new readers of the Bible that whenever they see the word "therefore" they should ask: "What is the "therefore" *there for?*" It is a good rule for Bible study.

Here, Paul is saying, "Because of what I have told you about the wisdom of God, don't get discouraged." But why should they be discouraged? "Because of my sufferings" is Paul's answer. You can see his thought pattern. He was in prison; perhaps the Christians were thinking: "If our leader has been silenced, what is the point in our plodding on?" They were discouraged. The word is used in extra-biblical Greek for the exhaustion of a woman in labor, who is just so physically drained she feels she cannot go on.

But look at how Paul is encouraging them. "You are talking as though I were a prisoner of Caesar. But I am only that superficially. In fact I am a 'prisoner for Jesus Christ,' and the reason I am in prison is 'for the sake of you Gentiles.' My suffering is not pointless; God has a plan to fulfill through it. My sufferings, in God's wisdom, are 'for you' and for 'your glory.'"

So, what is the "therefore" there for in Ephe-

sians 3:13? Paul is really saying, "Since you have
seen the wisdom of God in the foundation and
fellowship of the Church, will you trust the Lord's
wisdom in your trials, even when you cannot see
His wisdom or understand what His purpose is? If
the Lord has placed me here in prison, it *must be*
because He has some wise design in view. Surely
you can trust Him!"

In chapter one, we saw that the knowledge of
God demands patience and perseverance. Here is
a case in point: Perhaps at the time Paul wrote this
he did not yet know himself what God would do.
He had to learn to persevere, patiently waiting for
the Lord to work. As a matter of fact, the Lord did
work. In the Letter to the Philippians, Paul tells us
one of the effects of his imprisonment:

> Now I want you to know, brothers, that what
> has happened to me has really *served to advance
> the gospel. As a result,* it has become clear
> throughout the whole palace guard and to eve-
> ryone else *that I am in chains for Christ. Because
> of my chains,* most of the brothers in the Lord
> *have been encouraged* to speak the word of God
> more courageously and fearlessly. (Philippians
> 1:12-14)

Picture this scene on a cosmic scale. The
prison door shuts behind Paul. He is Caesar's
prisoner. The Church begins to lose heart. Perhaps the angels again hold their breath—What is
the Lord doing, allowing His leading witness to be
imprisoned and apparently silenced? The demonic

"rulers and authorities" clap their hands with glee: Paul is silenced, a battle has been won in the war against Heaven. There is joy in Hell!

But, see what *God* is doing! Soldiers come and go from guarding the prisoner. They notice he is no ordinary prisoner. He is here because of his faith in Jesus Christ. The guards who watch the prisoner are captive listeners to his bold witness. The word spreads through the whole palace guard! Clearly, God wanted the gospel to reach them too, and what better way to accomplish it than this! Soon the Church hears, and realizes that God is at work, and is encouraged to serve Him with greater boldness than ever. Surely the "foolishness of God" is wiser (and more effective) than the "wisdom of men"!

God's tapestry is being completed day by day; often we see only the rear view. Yes, we may detect some kind of pattern, but there are so many loose ends that the picture is not yet clear. But, Paul is saying, God gives you a glimpse of the front, the perfect weaving of the divine wisdom which will lead to "your glory" (Ephesians 3:13). That is why you should trust His wisdom implicitly, even when you do not fully understand it. Look again and again at the Church—at its foundation in the work of Christ, and its fellowship, and its sufferings—and be encouraged!

Who are the men and women whose lives are patterns of God's wisdom? They are those who, like Paul, can say they are not prisoners of circumstance, but prisoners of Jesus Christ. They are not living for themselves, but are devoted to the blessing of others. That is the canvas on which God paints His perfect design. It is those who have this kind of "heart for God" who can sing: "We may trust him fully, all for us to do; they who trust him wholly, find him wholly true."

No wonder Paul himself turned to doxology as he thought about these things, and prayed, "Now to him *who is able to do immeasurably more than all we ask or imagine,* according to his power that is at work within us, to him be glory *in the church and in Christ Jesus* throughout all generations, for ever and ever! Amen" (Ephesians 3:20-21). Should we not echo his "Amen"?

8
The Holy One of Israel

Words alone are incapable of teaching us what the holiness of God is. In men, true holiness means to be fully human. Holiness means being separate from sin; put positively, that means being whole, being what we ought to be—a true man or woman in God's image.

But God's holiness belongs to a different order of things. Yes, it means that God, too, is separate from sin. But holiness in God also means wholeness. God's holiness is His "God-ness." It is His being God in all that it means for Him to be God. To meet God in His holiness, therefore, is to be altogether overwhelmed by the discovery that He is God, and not man.

In our limited view of holiness, we tend to

associate it with certain sections of the Bible. We rightly think that Leviticus, for example, teaches us about holiness, in man and in God. But nowhere is the holiness of God more fully expounded than in the teaching and preaching of the prophet Isaiah. He knew the Lord as "The Holy One of Israel." On some thirty occasions Isaiah used that title for God.

Why did he do so? Probably because of a pattern that often occurs in the ministries of godly and outstanding leaders in the Church. The *burden* of his message, the focus of his thinking about the character of God, was shaped by the formative experiences that brought him into the knowledge of the Lord and the service of the Kingdom. For Isaiah, the knowledge of the Lord was fellowship with the Holy God. He had been in the presence of God, and seen holy creatures veil their faces before the infinitely greater holiness of God. He had heard them respond in overwhelming waves of worship to God: "Holy, holy, holy is the Lord Almighty; the whole earth is full of his glory" (Isaiah 6:3). That experience determined the whole course, and much of the content, of his ministry. If we examine it we will discover more of what it means to have a heart for the true God.

+   +   +

We know the exact year when the young prophet Isaiah met with God. It was 739 BC—"In the year that King Uzziah died" (Isaiah 6:1). Isaiah may have been in the Temple. But he was transported, spiritually, into the Heavenly Temple. There he saw the Lord enthroned in glory and majesty, worshiped unceasingly by the seraphs whose crescendo of praise caused the whole environment to shudder and shake. "Woe to me!" cried the prophet, "I am ruined! For I am a man of unclean lips, and I live among a people of unclean lips, and my eyes have seen the King, the LORD Almighty" (Isaiah 6:5).

Yet the *dating* of this event is not as significant as its *timing*. Isaiah underscores this fact when he describes the year in which he saw the Lord as "the year that King Uzziah died." To our ears that may sound unexceptional, but those words carry with them one of the great tragedies of Old Testament history.

Uzziah was the son of Amaziah. Amaziah was a king who "did what was right in the eyes of the Lord, but not wholeheartedly" (2 Chronicles 25:2). Unlike his father, Uzziah was determined to follow the Lord without compromise. "He sought God during the days of Zechariah, who instructed him in the fear of God. As long as he sought the LORD, God gave him success. . . . His fame spread far and wide, for he was greatly helped until he became powerful" (2 Chronicles 26:5,15). However, while Amaziah's weakness was compromising the Lord's standards, Uzziah's weakness was a failure to persevere in humility before God: "After Uzziah became powerful, his pride led to his downfall. He was unfaithful to the LORD his God, and entered the temple of the LORD to burn incense on the altar of incense" (2 Chronicles 26:16). Azariah the priest, along with eighty

others, bravely confronted and rebuked him. The
events that followed were doubtless at the fore-
front of Isaiah's mind throughout the year in
which he met with God.

> Uzziah, who had a censer in his hand ready to
> burn incense, became angry. While he was rag-
> ing at the priests in their presence before the
> incense altar in the Lord's temple, leprosy broke
> out on his forehead. When Azariah the chief
> priest and all the other priests looked at him,
> they saw that he had leprosy on his forehead, so
> they hurried him out. Indeed, he himself was
> eager to leave, because the Lord had afflicted
> him.
> *King Uzziah had leprosy until the day he
> died.* He lived in a separate house—leprous, and
> *excluded from the temple of the Lord.* (2 Chroni-
> cles 26:19-21)

Uzziah had come to the throne at the age of
sixteen. He had reigned for a half century. Great
expansion had taken place under his rule. He had
sought God, and God had notably blessed him. His
was a glorious reign, long enough to provide opportunity for prosperity and stability. But it was what
one commentator has called "the glorious reign
with the ghastly end." In his pride, Uzziah trans-
gressed God's holy laws. He showed that pride and
its resultant anger in the very place where God was
to be known as Lord: the Temple. He, too, encountered the holiness of God, and was chastised for his
sin and cut off from the means of grace.

Probably Isaiah was in the Temple himself when he had his great vision. Imagine what was going through his mind. Did he have an enthusiasm for Uzziah's policies that had just been painfully dashed? Why had he come to the Temple on this particular day? Was it a routine visit, or perhaps the anniversary of Uzziah's proud rebellion? Did Isaiah do what most of us would have done— wander around parts of the Temple thinking, "this is where Uzziah came that day, there is where he went in order to reach the incense altar. Here is where Azariah and the priests must have come . . ."? As he meditated on the sinfulness of man, as perhaps he meditated on some of his own sermons in which he had tried to expose the sinfulness of his contemporaries, he was overwhelmed with a sense of being lifted out of time into eternity; he was able to see through the Jerusalem Temple into the Heavenly Temple. There, like the Apostle John, he saw a throne—and seated upon the throne, the Living God before whom living creatures bow and "never stop saying: 'Holy, holy, holy is the Lord God Almighty, who was, and is, and is to come'" (Revelation 4:2,8).

Who can say exactly what thoughts were the springboard for Isaiah's experience? But what he tells us he saw is significant. He who had seen the demise of the earthly king in whom the nation had placed its hopes, and whose confidence in princes now lay shattered at his feet, saw *the King,* the Lord of Hosts! The experience completely and utterly devastated him.

In various ways Isaiah 6 is the biographical

parallel of the great courtroom scene in the opening three chapters of Romans. There Paul musters
all his evidence to show mankind its guilt. He
argues that men and women everywhere, Jew and
Gentile, are depraved and guilty before God.
Every part of man's being is corrupted. The whole
world deserves condemnation. As we stand before
the judgment seat, says Paul, *every mouth is shut.*
Proud men who have had so much to say for
themselves are stunned into silence. Those who
have protested their own righteousness find their
protests dying in their throats. Men discover what
they are: lost, broken, guilty, condemned sinners!
They must cry out with the psalmist: "If you, O
LORD, kept a record of sins, O LORD, who could
stand?" (Psalm 130:3; see Romans 3:9-19).

The same thing happened to Isaiah. All he
could do was confess his sinfulness before the
thrice holy God. "Woe to me!" was all he could
say. In the presence of the One before whom the
seraphs veiled their faces and covered their feet,
Isaiah came to a new self image altogether. He was
no longer the preacher who exposed the sinfulness
of the people. He was the servant, standing before
his Master, his sin exposed before His all-seeing,
all-knowing, all-holy gaze. Knowing God in this
way was, in the truest sense of the words, the most
awe-full moment in his life.

Scholars debate the precise point in Isaiah's
ministry at which this event took place. Many
suggest that what we have here is his initial call.
But a good case can be made for suggesting that
Isaiah was already a prophet, and that the con-

demnation of the people described in the previous
chapters of his prophecy was already characteristic of his ministry. If this is correct (which I rather
think it is), Isaiah was now learning the truth of
what he had already been preaching, discovering
the real burden of his message, and, most important of all, discovering the sinfulness of his own
heart.

This may be why the focus of Isaiah's confession is on the fact that *he* is "a man of unclean
lips." Surely, we might reason, the man had the
purest lips in Jerusalem. He had spoken God's
holy Word! Perhaps—but those God uses come to
recognize that they are the chief of sinners.
(1 Timothy 1:12-16). What Isaiah was actually
discovering was that even his best actions (preaching God's Word) were polluted and defiled. Far
from being "fit" to preach, he was by nature
utterly disqualified from doing so. It was his *righteous* acts that were like filthy rags (Isaiah 64:6).

Some Christians never seem to make this
discovery about themselves. They are never
brought to the place where they see that it is their
very "strengths" or "qualities" or "gifts" that
stand in need of cleansing from God. No discovery
could be more devastating. *And if the sense of the
presence of the Holy One of Israel does anything, it
devastates a man or woman.* Thus we become those
of whom Isaiah was later to say, in God's name,
"This is the one I esteem: he who is humble and
contrite in spirit, and trembles at my word"
(Isaiah 66:2).

There is a direct relationship between this

devastating sense of God's holiness and the quality of our Christian service. It puts a unique tone
into the way in which we respond to the call of
God, "Whom shall I send? And who will go for
us?" All kinds of people may say: "Here am I.
Send me!" But only the man or woman who has
bowed humbly before the Lord as Isaiah did
speaks in the tones that God delights to hear.

Today there is rampant a view of the Christian life which regards this kind of talk as *passe*.
After all, is Isaiah not describing the cringing
experience of the Old Testament, long before the
revelation of God's character in Jesus Christ?

That sounds very plausible, and may even
seem spiritual and biblical. Unfortunately, it con-
tradicts what Scripture explicitly says. In John's
Gospel, Isaiah 6:10 is quoted:

> He has blinded their eyes
>   and deadened their hearts,
> so they can neither see with their eyes,
>   nor understand with their hearts,
>   nor turn—and I would heal them.
>   (John 12:39-40)

There is nothing remarkable about this statement.
What is remarkable is *John's explanation of why
Isaiah said it:* "Isaiah said this because he saw
Jesus' glory and spoke about him" (John 12:41). It
was *Jesus* whom Isaiah encountered in the Tem-
ple. It was *Jesus* whom the seraphs worshiped as
the thrice-holy Lord. It was in the presence of
Jesus that Isaiah knew himself to be utterly sinful.

Nor was this an "Old Testament" experience. Remember Simon Peter's reaction to Jesus when, at Jesus' command, the disciples caught more fish than their nets could contain? "When Simon Peter saw this, he fell at Jesus' knees and said, 'Go away from me, Lord; I am a sinful man'" (Luke 5:8). What had happened to Peter was his discovery that his great natural strength (*he* was a *fisherman, Jesus* was a *carpenter*!) was not strength and knowledge, but weakness and ignorance! And, lest we think (wrongly) that this was just a display of emotionalism on Peter's part, think of John's experience: "When I saw him [Jesus], I fell at his feet as though dead" (Revelation 1:17).

Is this the Christ you know? It should be, because there is no other Christ than this one. He is a *Holy* Savior.

But what impression did this leave on Isaiah, and what should we expect that encounter with the Holy One of Israel will do in shaping our lives?

First, we will realize that *the holiness of God is the total integrity of His being*. To encounter Him in His holiness is to be overwhelmed by God. Christians in this century have sometimes spoken of being "broken before God." That *almost* expresses what Scripture means, but not quite. For God does not "break" His children ("A bruised reed he will not break, and a smoldering wick he will not snuff out" was how Isaiah later described the Servant of the Lord—Isaiah 42:3). Rather, what we experience is more akin to being "dismantled." The sheer power of God's holy presence—His "unapproachable light" (1 Timothy

6:16)—penetrates to the secret faults, the unknown inconsistencies, the moral weaknesses, the spiritual compromises of our lives: "Nothing in all creation is hidden from God's sight. Everything is uncovered and laid bare before the eyes of him to whom we must give account," and the proof of this is found in the impact of God's Word. It is "living and active. Sharper than any double-edged sword, it penetrates even to dividing soul and spirit, joints and marrow; it judges *the thoughts and attitudes of the heart*" (Hebrews 4:12-13).

What we come to realize in God's holy presence is that we are what our spiritual forefathers called "totally depraved." We may not be "as bad as we might be." But the point is that *no part* of our lives is free from the pollution of sin. There is spiritual down-drag everywhere. Our sinfulness sets up spiritual "G-forces," which influence every single action and motivation. In the presence of the Holy One of Israel, we can only say, as Paul discovered, "I am unspiritual, sold as a slave to sin. . . . What a wretched man I am!" (Romans 7:14,24).

Isaiah saw this pervasiveness of sin in the people. That is why his preaching sought to strip away the veneer of their lives and show them how they really looked before God. Their whole body was injured, their heart afflicted; from the soles of their feet to the top of their head, "there is no soundness—only wounds and welts and open sores, not cleansed or bandaged or soothed with oil" (Isaiah 1:6). In fact, unless God had shown His mercy, Isaiah said, "we would have become like Sodom, we would have been like Gomorrah" (Isaiah 1:9).

Do you see the significance of what Isaiah was saying? He was castigating the people for their sin, but what he discovered in the Temple was that he was utterly sinful himself. His own natural condition was hopeless, unless God had mercy on him. As God's servant, he was now discovering the extent of sin's influence in his own life. He learned this in the presence of the Holy One.

+   +   +

The immediate repercussion of this recognition of God's holiness is that, second, *all self-deception is challenged.* We see how easily we have misread our true spiritual failure, how superficially we have thought about our relationship to God. We have rather casually compared ourselves with others, and received at least a passing grade in our own estimation. But now, before God, we are "undeceived." We discover, as did the young Scottish preacher of the nineteenth century, Robert Murray M'Cheyne, that in our hearts there lie the seeds of every known sin. Only upbringing, environment, and the restraints of society prevent us from running headlong into sins of enormous proportions.

Who knows the extent to which we would give in to sin, were we to be given a guarantee of immunity from discovery and exposure?

I once had the privilege of participating in a conference with an author and speaker who was also a qualified psychiatrist. He gave an address that had an impact I have never forgotten, for two reasons. One was the number of people I met afterwards who had been disturbed by it (which was, I thought, precisely what they should have been; and, I suspected, the right and necessary intention of the speaker). The other indelible impression was the quiet, but altogether realistic, way in which he had conducted a dissection of Christian man in all his frailty and sinfulness. The speaker had catalogued some of the moral failures of individuals, and provided statistics that unveiled the readiness with which Christians will compromise morally when they believe themselves to be unobserved and unobservable. His address was totally controlled and rational; there were no hystrionics, just insistent, devastating analysis of Christians. He offered no cheap grace, only painful realities. Perhaps his findings partly explain the reaction: we find it so difficult to face up to a basic fact of our identity—our depravity and defilement of the glorious image of God.

I confess I had to struggle to control the breaking up of the wells of my emotions. I wanted to weep and weep—for the Church, for fellow Christians I had known to fall into public sin, for the conference I was attending, lest we fail to hear the prophetic note in what was being said, for myself, in all my own moral weakness and frailty.

Now, why was this evening so devastating? There was no attempt to play on emotions. But in all that was said, I discerned a pattern: here was Christian man, as he is, viewed from the perspective of God's holiness. We had been given knowledge of God and of ourselves. We had been confronted with our moral disintegration, not our emotional "brokenness." I for one felt close to Isaiah's cry: "*Woe to me! I am ruined!* For I am a man of unclean lips. . . and my eyes have seen the King, the Lord Almighty." Isaiah was right: we are moral ruins, and only by the grace of God are we daily preserved from total self-destruction.

When the dawn of this day of God's holiness breaks upon our spirits, we are delivered from all superficial and inadequate thoughts about our own sanctification. We are also preserved from any cheap teaching that encourages us to think that there are shortcuts by which we may more easily obtain holiness. Holiness is not an experience; it is the re-integration of our character, the rebuilding of a ruin. It is skilled labor, a long-term project, demanding everything God has given us for life and godliness.

The discovery of God's holiness teaches us that we can no longer serve Him by the transformation of life's externals (significant though that may sometimes be). We see now that we must deal with sin for what it is, and "put to death" what belongs to the flesh:

> *Put to death,* therefore, whatever belongs to
> your earthly nature [the flesh]: sexual immoral
> ity, impurity, lust, evil desires and greed, which
> is idolatry. . . . Now *you must rid yourselves* of
> all such things as these: anger, rage, malice,
> slander, and filthy language from your lips. Do
> not lie to each other, since you have taken off

your old self with its practices and have put on
the new self. . . .

Therefore, *as God's chosen people, holy* and
dearly loved, clothe yourselves with compassion,
kindness, humility, gentleness and patience.
Bear with each other. . . . (Colossians 3:5-13)

The holiness of God teaches us that there is
only one way to deal with sin—radically, seriously,
painfully, constantly. If you do not so live, you do
not live in the presence of the Holy One of Israel.

+   +   +

The discovery of God's holiness has a third profound impact on our lives: *We enter into a deeper
awareness of the blessings of forgiveness.* This impact
was certainly true for Isaiah. He saw one of the
seraphs flying towards him, as soon as he had
confessed his terrible guilt and pollution. He carried a coal—*in his hand*—lifted with tongs from
the altar of fire and sacrifice in the Temple. With
the burning coal, he touched Isaiah's mouth!
Think of the sharpness of the pain. Think, too, of
the appropriateness of the action for the man of
unclean lips. "See," said the seraph, "this has
touched your lips; your guilt is taken away and
your sin atoned for" (Isaiah 6:7).

Isaiah experienced this purification in a vision.
But in effect his vision was a preview of the Cross.
There, too, the holiness of God became *visible,* in
the darkness of judgment that surrounded our
Lord on Calvary; there, too, it became *audible,* as
on the Cross He bore the sins of His people—as

though He said, "I stand in the place of the man with unclean lips and the people with unclean lips," as He cried out, "My God, my God, I am forsaken. Why?" God there unveiled how holy He is, judging His own Son when His Son appeared before Him in the robes of man's sinfulness.

Yet, from the altar of the Cross, Another Seraph flies to us. This One is the Spirit of Burnings. He brings us fire from the altar of Calvary, by which our sins are forgiven and cleansed. In the rediscovery of our sinfulness we learn what it means: "those who are forgiven much, love much." And we discover that the foundation of our love for the Lord lies in the recognition of His holiness, our sinfulness, and His grace.

+   +   +

All this effect of his encounter with the Holy One prepared Isaiah for his ministry. He who has gazed at his own sinfulness will be able to persevere in the face of setbacks. He will not be surprised by the sins of those to whom he ministers; he will grieve over them. He will weep for the sins of his companions as well as his own sins; but he will not despair because of them, for he has a *realistic* view of himself, not a superficial one. What is more, he has a glorious view of God, and of His power to save and to keep. The man who has seen little of his own sin will be little acquainted with the wonders of grace. The man who has gazed on his own heart with God-given illumination, and who has seen the grace of Christ in that light, is the one who, loving much, will give much.

What we know of God determines the ministry and service we render. Perhaps nowhere is this truth more critical than at this point: *He who would know what fruitfulness is must know what God's holiness is.*

9
The Faithful Provider

The providence of God is the way in which He governs everything wisely, first for the glory of His own Name, and second for the ultimate blessing of His children. Clearly, the providence of God is closely connected with the wisdom of God. We need to be confident that all things *work together* for our good, if we are to be able to cope with what seem to us to be the "not-goods" of life. This is why the Bible teaches us in many different ways that every event of life, every circumstance of each day, is guided by the hand of our Father. He has numbered the hairs on our heads (Matthew 10:30). No detail of our lives is outside of His purpose or control.

This thought causes some Christians difficul-

ties, and makes them ask, "If I were to believe that
God is universally in control in His providence in
the world, wouldn't that paralyze me, and make
me think that nothing I did really mattered?" In
fact, as the lives of many Christians demonstrate—and as the life of the Lord Jesus Christ
most clearly shows—believing in God's complete
providence and control has the opposite effect.
Instead of discouraging us, it encourages us! That,
after all, is why God has taught us about His
providence in His Word! We know that nothing
(trouble, hardship, persecution, famine, nakedness, peril, sword—all elements in the world
which God providentially rules) can ever separate
us from the love of God in Christ. *How* do we
know that? Paul's answer is that we know that God
has a purpose *through* these things. He is *for us*
(Romans 8:31), and therefore, ultimately, none of
our difficult circumstances can be against us.
They serve God's purpose, and must therefore
serve our blessing.

We can study the Bible's teaching on God's
providence in various ways. We could, for example, take an overview of the whole of biblical teaching on the theme, bring it together in a more or less
systematic form, and examine it in that way. Each
biblical doctrine is a multi-faceted jewel, and we
can learn a great deal by trying to understand all its
different facets.

Alternatively, we could focus on one of the
great statements Scripture makes about providence. Romans 8:28, for example, would make an
excellent study. Beginning with the fact that God

works everything together for our good in accordance with His purpose, we could reflect on what His purpose *is*, and on the different ways He seems to be bringing it to pass in our own lives. Again, that would be a perfectly legitimate procedure, and would prove to be very instructive.

There is, however, a third way of tackling the providence of God, and that is by tracing it *biographically* through the life of a character in Scripture. Several people in the Bible would provide outstanding illustrations. Joseph is one: Remember how, as he looked back on his experience, he could say to his brothers, "You intended to harm me, but God intended it for good to accomplish what is now being done, the saving of many lives. So then, don't be afraid. I will provide for you and your children" (Genesis 50:19-20). Joseph's promise to provide for the families of his brothers is based on his knowledge that God provided for him, to bring blessing to his life and to others through him. What his brothers did was genuinely significant—and hurt Joseph deeply. But Joseph had eyes to see that God was also at work, and that His purposes had been fulfilled *not just in spite of his brothers,* but even *through their actions*!

We could trace the same pattern in Paul's life. Think, for example, of the extended narrative in Acts, from the moment Paul appeals to Caesar until the time he arrives in Rome (Acts 26:10-28:31). All of these events fulfill Paul's God-given desire to preach the gospel at Rome also (Romans 1:13). But they also illustrate how, each step of his way, God was in control and provided opportunities for Paul to witness to Christ that would not have existed otherwise.

The most overlooked example of God's providence is in the life and ministry of Jesus Himself. Here is the perfect example of one whose whole life was under the control of the heavenly Father, who encountered opposition, pain, disappointment, and ultimately rejection—yet those very things were the means God used to fulfill His perfect plan. So at least Simon Peter saw on the Day of Pentecost: "This man was handed over to you by God's set purpose and foreknowledge; and you, with the help of wicked men, put him to death by nailing him to the cross. But God raised him from the dead, freeing him from the agony of death, because it was impossible for death to keep its hold on him" (Acts 23-24). Here two things are placed side by side: 1) the reality of men's evil deeds and Jesus' suffering; and 2) the plan of God carried out through those very deeds. There, indeed, is God's providence. There, too, in Jesus' free and willing obedience to His Father, we see that God's sovereign purpose did not deny His sense of responsibility—it encouraged it.

Joseph and Paul and Jesus are relatively obvious examples of God's providence at work. There is, however, a less obvious, but equally clear, example tucked away in the Old Testament book of Ruth. Naomi, Ruth's mother-in-law, is a rather different, but no less valuable, illustration of the wonderful ways God rules and provides to bring about His purpose.

In some ways Naomi is an especially valuable

example. She is a woman, and experienced the great principles of God's grace in circumstances with which women can particularly identify. What is more, her life illustrates a great principle of God's providence: His work in our lives usually begins with His work in somebody else's life. Although the Book of Ruth is really about Ruth, its first chapter (which is mainly about Naomi) teaches us that what God planned to accomplish in and through Ruth really began with what He did in and through Naomi!

+ + +

The Book of Ruth is set against the background of the days of the Judges, when "Israel had no king; everyone did as he saw fit" (Judges 21:25). The Book of Judges traces the rebellion of God's people against Him, and the provision He made for them by delivering them from the consequences of their folly, in order to fulfill His purposes in them. It is the story of the nation God delivered and protected, "like an eagle that stirs up its nest and hovers over its young, that spreads its wings to catch them and carries them on its pinions" (Exodus 32:11). In a sense, Ruth is a story about the same God doing the same thing, but in a *family* rather than a *national* context. The message of the book is summed up by the words of Boaz to Ruth that have the same imagery: "May you be richly rewarded by the LORD, the God of Israel, under whose wings you have come to take refuge" (Ruth 2:12). To take refuge under the Lord's wings is simply another way of describing the experience of God's salvation and providence. It is what

Psalm 91 calls dwelling "in the shelter of the Most High" and resting "in the shadow of the Almighty." Our confidence then is: "He will cover you with his feathers, and under his wings you will find refuge; his faithfulness will be your shield and rampart. . . ." This is what it means to say, "I will say of the LORD, 'He is my refuge and my fortress, my God, in whom I trust'" (Psalm 91:1,4,2).

Naomi discovered this refuge under God's wings through some very dark experiences, and in situations which are difficult to understand. But when we place them in a large context, four lessons become clear. *First,* God's providences at times are painful and severe; *second,* through these experiences He may touch the lives of others; *third,* He brings us to an appreciation of His ways with us that we would otherwise lack; and *fourth,* He fulfills His purposes through us in ways that far exceed our expectations.

Each of these features of divine providence is etched in the life of Naomi.

Consider the catalog of personal sorrow and tragedy with which the Book of Ruth opens:

> In the days when the judges ruled, there was a famine in the land, and a man from Bethlehem in Judah, together with his wife and two sons, went to live for a while in the country of Moab. The man's name was Elimelech, his wife's name Naomi, and the names of his two sons were Mahlon and Kilion. They were Ephrathites from Bethlehem, Judah. And they went to Moab and lived there.

Now Elimelech, Naomi's husband, died,
and she was left with her two sons. They married Moabite women, one named Orpah and the
other Ruth. After they had lived there about ten
years, both Mahlon and Kilion also died, and
Naomi was left without her two sons and her
husband. (Ruth 1:1-5)

Devastating, isn't it? All the more so when we
read the passage with sensitivity to the symbolism
expressed in the names of the characters.

Here is a young woman with two sons. Her
own name means "Pleasant." But nothing pleasant is said about her life. Her boys' names reveal a
secret burden she apparently bore from the moment
of their birth, for Mahlon means "Weakling" and
Kilion means "Pining." As time confirms, their
lives may have seemed to hang in the balance from
their earliest hours. Only a mother who has daily
feared for her children's well-being can fully
appreciate the extended shadow this apprehension
cast across Naomi's path.

Naomi's husband, by contrast, has a glorious
name, Elimelech (*El-i* = My God; *melech* = King).
Yet when God's people come under His judgment
and there is a famine in the land (perhaps like the
situation described in Judges 6:1-6), instead of
turning to the Lord in repentance for the sins of
the people, Elimelech turns away from the land in
which God has promised to bless and keep His
people, and makes his way "to live for a while" in
the land of Moab.

There is something perfectly understandable

about leaving a troubled land. Many a man has emigrated in order to make a better life for himself and his family. There is nothing inherently wrong with emigration! However, there was something spiritually sinister about Elimelech's action, because he was leaving God's land, and thereby turning away from the promises God had given. In keeping with his name, he should instead have been looking to God to forgive his people and restore their fortunes. This is underlined in the family's intention to spend only a short time in Moab ("to live for a while," verse 1). Yet at least ten years elapsed before there was any sign of a return. By that time both the father and the two boys lay buried in Moabite graves.

We cannot say how responsible Naomi herself was for these decisions—although it is an unusual marriage in which the wife has no say at all! Nor do we need to pronounce on the extent to which the deaths of the three men represent some kind of judgment on their lives. What is obvious is that these experiences represent an unusual catalog of sorrow in the life of one woman. It is one thing to be widowed; another thing to be widowed in a foreign land; and yet another for a widow to see the fruit of her own womb snatched prematurely from her by death. Doubtless the second bereavement doubled the sorrow of the first, and the third bereavement made Naomi feel the world had become not only empty, but numbingly dark. She was cut off from the past by emigration, cut off from the present by the loss of her husband, cut off from the future by the deaths of her sons before they could become fathers.

Faced with such severe providences in her life, Naomi had two choices: to turn *away* from God and toward her own despair; or to turn *to* God and away from her despair. She did the latter: She turned to the Lord and returned to His people. She heard that in mercy He had come to the aid of His people (Ruth 1:6). She knew that she too needed His aid, and so she set off for Bethlehem.

We cannot pass final judgment on all the details of God's hand on Naomi's life and experience, but one thing is clear: Through these dark experiences, every possible substitute for God in her life was removed, every potential barrier was broken down. Through this catalog of tragedy, God was restoring Naomi to Himself.

This restoration is always the purpose of God's providential governing of His children's lives. We may think that such severity is inconsistent with what we know of God's gentleness and compassion. But that is because we do not appreciate how seriously God loves us, and how determined He is that we should have His best, even if it means pain. In Naomi's case, those pains of providence are written in capital letters. But God wrote them like that partly to help us read what He writes in our lives, in small letters and sometimes even in shorthand. The message is the same: *He will stop at nothing to bless us!* In a nutshell, that is what the providence of God really means.

+ + +

There is more to God's providence in Naomi's

experience, however, than her personal restoration. The exquisite narrative of Ruth 1 goes on to describe the journey on which Naomi was accompanied by her daughters-in-law Orpah and Ruth. They arrived at the crossroads between Moab and Bethlehem—a "point of no return." Naomi told them to return to their own homes. She prayed that they would find the blessings of new husbands, home, and family among their own people (a fact that made the commentator Matthew Henry remark, somewhat wryly, that the prayers of a mother-in-law are not to be despised!). The girls assured her they would remain with her.

But then, something new happened: Naomi spoke more directly to them about *the cost* involved in going with her to the Lord's people. It might mean her daughters-in-law would have to stay single for the rest of their lives. That challenge, profound as it is today, was all the more so then, when a woman depended on marriage to provide for her throughout life.

What was so remarkable about Naomi's speech? For the first time in these past ten years, Naomi was spiritually equipped to challenge others about the cost of discipleship—because she was paying it herself! Since she was no longer merely a *sufferer,* but was now a *disciple* (or at least a returning penitent), her daughters-in-law could *see* in her life the character of the discipleship to which they aspired. What she said about its cost made sense to them now.

One of the daughters-in-law returned to Moab. But the other one, Ruth, went on to

Bethlehem with Naomi. She said to her mother-in-law:

> Don't urge me to leave you or to turn back from you. Where you go I will go, and where you stay I will stay. Your people will be my people and your God my God. Where you die I will die, and there I will be buried. May the Lord deal with me, be it ever so severely, if anything but death separates you and me. (Ruth 1:16-17)

Ruth's words are often read as the perfect expression of loyalty from one woman to another. They do express such loyalty, very beautifully. But to see *only* that in them is to misread them, for they express a higher loyalty—as a little awareness of biblical language shows. Ruth is really confessing her conversion and trust in the Lord. That is why her words often remind us of the words in which God characteristically confirmed His covenant with His people: "I will be your God, and you will be my people" (Leviticus 26:12; see also Exodus 6:7; Jeremiah 11:4 and 30:3). Ruth is taking hold of God's covenant promise of grace and provision for His people, and she is saying, "I give myself to this God of yours, Naomi, and I bind myself to those who are His people and your people—all my life!"

Here, in part, is the explanation of the darkness through which Naomi had gone. Just as God's means to reach Roman soldiers was to permit Paul's imprisonment, so in order to bring Ruth into His Kingdom He worked through Naomi's sorrows. What seemed to be His special providence in Naomi's life was *also* His special providence in Ruth's life. God is always at least one step ahead of us in His calculations!

Yet usefulness in God's hands is not necessarily the same as having a heart for God Himself. Sometimes the Lord uses us despite ourselves. It is simply not biblical to say He will not "use" us unless we are obedient to Him and living in the fullness of the Spirit. He may "use" us even when our hearts are not attuned to Him. He works out His own plans in His own way. But He loves to use those who have a heart to love and serve Him, and the closing verses of Ruth 1 indicate that Naomi had such a heart.

At the marketplace in Bethlehem, the ladies gathered to share the gossip of the day. On everyone's lips was the return of Naomi and her daughter-in-law Ruth. "Is it really Naomi?" some of them asked; she seemed so different—not just older, but changed, somehow.

The change was not such as the passage of time alone produces. It was deeper; spiritual in character. It set the town buzzing. Sometimes one has the privilege of seeing this kind of phenomenon—a Christian's life so changed, so restored, perhaps, that people cannot stop talking about it. I remember being asked about such a change in someone I knew—by someone who was a total stranger, both to me and to the person whose life had been transformed. She had heard from others of "the change that had taken place" in someone in another town. "Do you know. . . ? Is it true, what

I've heard—about the change?" That kind of transformation is a glorious thing to see. It had happened to Naomi. And now she wanted to explain it. This change was due to God's hand, God's providence.

John Flavel, one of the great Puritan preachers in England in the seventeenth century, once said that the providence of God is like a Hebrew word—it can only be read backwards! That is what we find Naomi doing here: she confesses the providences of God in her life, which she is now just beginning to understand.

Naomi has three things to say. "Don't call me Naomi, call me Mara, because the Lord has made my life very bitter." Do not misread those words. Naomi does not say that *she* is bitter in spirit, but that *life* has been bitter. There is a world of difference in this distinction. The person who has a heart for God may have a bitter life without developing a bitter heart. Naomi is saying, "I want my name changed"—from "Pleasant" to "Bitter"— "to testify to the need for God to send bitter experiences to me to make my life sweet. My life has not been pleasant, but bitter; but I want the rest of my life to testify to what God can do through such bitter experiences."

The second part of Naomi's testimony to the providence of God was, "I went away full, but the Lord has brought me back empty." The family's journey to Moab in a time of famine would seem to suggest that "full" means "full of ourselves, our hopes, our plans," rather than materially prosperous. If so, Naomi had indeed returned "empty."

Her family had been snatched from her; her pride had been destroyed. She had nothing. She could not be sure that she would receive anything but contempt in the eyes of her neighbors. Yet the great thing she saw was that the Lord had brought her back—to His land, His people, and Himself.

Then, thirdly, Naomi draws the logical conclusion of what she has just been saying. We would hesitate to say it about her, but she says it about herself: "The LORD has afflicted me, the Almighty has brought misfortune upon me." Yet at the heart of this confession, wrung from her lips at such great cost, lies "the LORD" (she uses His covenant name, *Yahweh*). Here lay her security, although she had nothing; here lay her hope in a desperate situation: The Lord had refused to let go of her. As the Shepherd of His sheep, He had sent His sheepdogs of sorrow and affliction to bring her home. Now she had returned to the fold. She would have been able to say: "Before I was afflicted I went astray, but now I obey your word" (Psalm 119:67).

Yet even this restoration is an inadequate explanation for all of Naomi's experiences. We instinctively feel that there must be something more. When a grain of wheat falls into the ground and dies, said Jesus, it bears much fruit (John 12:24). Is there not a similar pattern in Naomi's experience? Indeed there is, but we have to turn further on in Scripture to find it.

Have you ever read right to the end of the Book of Ruth? To our Western minds it has a strange, anticlimactic conclusion—a family tree:

Perez was the father of Hezron
Hezron the father of Ram,
Ram the father of Amminadab,
Amminadab the father of Nahshon,
Nahshon the father of Salmon,
Salmon the father of Boaz,
Boaz [Ruth's husband] the father of Obed,
Obed the father of Jesse,
and Jesse the father of *David*.

(Ruth 4:18-21)

Do you see the significance of this family tree? Try to think of it this way: What was God planning as He oversaw Naomi's emigration, the tragic death of her husband, the marriage of her son to Ruth, the death of both of her sons, and the long, humbling trek home to Bethlehem? Not simply Naomi's spiritual restoration, or Ruth's conversion and later marriage to Boaz, nor even the happiness of Ruth becoming a mother and Naomi a grandmother (at last!). Yes, those were gracious fruits of His providence—but God was planning much more. He was planning the family tree, and the family influences, of the life of great King David!

But we must go even further. For Ruth's genealogy is found elsewhere in Scripture—in the opening chapter of the New Testament, where David's genealogy is repeated. But there it is not *David's* genealogy; it is the family tree of our Lord and Savior Jesus Christ! That, ultimately, was what God was planning. That is the final explanation for the mystery of God's providence in Naomi's life. Humanly speaking, God was planning untold blessing for mankind. He was digging down deeply. Centuries before the Incarnation, He was calling into His purposes the suffering of Naomi!

> Deep in unfathomable mines
> Of never failing skill,
> He treasures up His bright designs
> And works His sovereign will.

What God did on a large scale in Naomi's life, He continues to do in miniature in His providence in our lives. His purposes in the immediate future are wrapped up in our response to His providences in the present. But generations beyond our own will be affected by our response to Him as well. For God has called us into His Kingdom, to the center of His purposes. What a privilege this is! For the man or woman who has a heart for God, this is one of the most glorious truths of all—that in His wisdom and rule, God does far more than anything we could ever ask or think:

> *Judge not the Lord by feeble strength,*
> *But trust Him for His grace.*
> *Behind a frowning providence*
> *He hides a smiling face.*
> *William Cowper*

10
Let Us
Worship God!

In the churches I was reared in as a child, every service in probably every congregation began with the same four words. I suppose my grandfather heard them at the beginning of the services he attended, and his grandfather before him. They are not heard quite so often now, but they perfectly express what the service is for. They also express what our study in previous chapters should produce in our hearts.

Those words are, *"Let us worship God."* A.W. Tozer once called worship "the missing jewel of the evangelical church." He was almost entirely right. We have fine buildings with their wonderful facilities; we have classes and organizations, both inside and outside of our churches. We

have Christian literature, tapes and records of
Christian music, videos, conferences, seminars
and seminaries—and yet one is left asking: *Do we
worship the Lord with greater skill, in fresh joy and
intensity, because of these things?* Of course they are
good and valuable in themselves; that is not really
the issue. The issue is whether they have brought
us, or whether we have allowed ourselves to be
brought, to the heart of the matter: the worship of
God for which we were created and for which we
have been redeemed by His grace.

Where God is at the center of things, worship
inevitably follows. Where there is no spirit of worship, there God has been dethroned and dis-
placed. If what we have learned together so far
about the character of God should do anything in
us, it should lead us to worship. That was one of
Paul's great concerns for the church at Corinth,
which was so taken up with lesser issues. His
longing was that when a stranger came into their
midst and heard the Word of God proclaimed
among them, he would fall down on his face and
confess in worship, "God is really among you"
(1 Corinthians 11:25). But that was happening as
infrequently in Corinth as it does among our own
congregations today. Why? Because secondary
concerns have blinded the eyes of the Church to its
real function: to worship God.

In reply we might well say that the Church
exists—we exist—for other things. True enough:
But our problem is not our lack of other concerns.
Rather, our problem is that we fail, too, in so many
of these other concerns (evangelism, church fel-

lowship, social action) because we have failed so
miserably in this central concern: We do not worship the Lord as we should. One of our great
needs, therefore, towards the close of our study of
the character of God, is to think more seriously
and carefully about worship.

That is precisely what the ninety-second
Psalm was written to encourage. It has the title,
"A song. For the Sabbath day." It was written,
obviously, by someone who had come to a more
profound appreciation of what it means to worship
God. As a result he shared his experience in this
great poem, in which he opens his heart to the
Lord and exemplifies the spirit of praise and ado-
ration. Presumably it is "For the Sabbath day" to
give instruction and encouragement to the people
of God as they give themselves on that day more
freely and fully to worship.

The Psalm covers four areas of concern—the
basis, the blessings, the character, and the fruit of
true spiritual worship.

> It is good to praise the LORD and make music to
> your name, O Most High,
> to proclaim your love in the morning and your
> faithfulness at night,
> to the music of the ten-stringed lyre and the
> melody of the harp.
>
> For you make me glad by your deeds, O LORD;
> I sing for joy at the work of your hands.
> How great are your works, O LORD, how pro-
> found your thoughts!

The senseless man does not know, fools do not
  understand,
that though the wicked spring up like grass and
  all evildoers flourish,
they will be forever destroyed.

But you, O LORD, are exalted forever.

For surely your enemies, O LORD, surely your
  enemies will perish; all evildoers will be
  scattered.
You have exalted my horn like that of a wild ox;
  fine oils have been poured upon me.
My eyes have seen the defeat of my adversaries;
  my ears have heard the rout of my wicked
  foes.

The righteous will flourish like a palm tree, they
  will grow like a cedar of Lebanon;
planted in the house of the LORD, they will
  flourish in the courts of our God.
They will still bear fruit in old age, they will stay
  fresh and green,
proclaiming, "The LORD is upright; he is my
  Rock, and there is no wickedness in him.
                                            (Psalm 92)

It is a beautiful psalm, isn't it?

The *basis of worship* in these words is obvious.
The worship of the psalmist is the direct consequence of the God-centeredness of his heart and
life. His lips make music and are full of praise
(verse 1). But notice that he is not interested in the

music for its own sake, nor even because of its influence on his emotions, beneficial though that may be. No! What dominates his thinking is that his praise is directed *to the Lord,* and his music is made "to your name, O Most High." That is the difference between going to a service "for the worship" and going to a service "to worship the Lord." The distinction appears to be a minor one, but it may imply the difference between the worship of God and the worship of music!

The foundation of worship in the heart, therefore, is not *emotional* ("I feel full of worship" or "The atmosphere is so worshipful"). Actually, it is *theological.* Worship is not something we "work up"; it is something that "comes down" to us, from the character of God.

There is a beautiful illustration of this origin of worship in Psalm 133, which describes the blessing of Christian fellowship in days of worship. This psalm is one of a series of psalms, fifteen in all, which have the title "song of ascents." They form a kind of "hymns for special occasions" section in the psalter, and were used when the people went on pilgrimage to Jerusalem. They convey the expectations and blessings of the Lord's people at such a time. Like Christians today, the Old Testament believers found these "conferences" rich times of worship and fellowship. In Psalm 133 the author tries to describe in word-pictures what those times were like.

The first picture he uses is of the oil of anointing, which was poured on to the head of the High Priest, flowing down his beard and onto his robes.

The second picture he uses is the dew, which falls on faraway Mount Hermon, falling instead on Jerusalem.

What do these pictures mean? In both cases the emphasis lies on the oil and the dew "coming down"—down from God, who anoints His priests for service and sends the dew in the world of nature. "There the Lord bestows his blessing," says the psalmist in conclusion (Psalm 133:3). It is God who gives us the spirit of worship, and it is *what we know of God* that produces this spirit of worship. We might say that worship is simply theology, doctrine, what we think about God, going into top gear! Instead of merely thinking about Him, we tell Him, in prayer and praise and song, how great and glorious we believe Him to be!

We find this acclamation spelled out in Psalm 92. The writer is full of God. He talks about God's *grace*: His "love in the morning," His "faithfulness at night" are the themes of his songs. He is awed by the mighty works of God, both in creation and providence, in redemption and preservation. God's "deeds" make him glad, the "works of his hands" make him sing for joy. As he contemplates what God has revealed in His Word, he is awestruck by the profound character of God's thoughts (verse 5). He thinks, too, about the ways in which God has delivered him from opposition: "you have exalted my horn [the symbol of strength]" (verse 10). In the world at large, in the history of God's people, in the Scriptures, in personal experience, he has found God to be at the center.

No wonder he cries out with joy, "You, O LORD, are exalted forever"! Like other believers in the Old Testament period, he had a sense of the Lord being enthroned on the praises of His people. He had seen a measure of the glory of his God. Here was a man who was prepared to let God be God!

Too often we fail to appreciate that this apprehension of God is not only the test of our worship, but also the test of our spiritual growth. A Christian's real development in spiritual life will always be revealed by how he or she thinks about God—how much he thinks about Him, and how highly he thinks about Him. For *worship* is, essentially, the reverse of sin. Sin began (and begins) when we succumb to the temptation, "You shall be as gods." We make ourselves the center of the universe and dethrone God. By contrast, worship is giving God His true *worth*; it is acknowledging Him to be the Lord of all things, and the Lord of everything in our lives. He is, indeed, the Most High God!

+ + +

Psalm 92 also describes *the blessings of worship.* "It is good to praise the LORD and make music to your name, O Most High" (verse 1).

At first glance that wording may seem to represent the view of "old fashioned medicine" that regularly appears on television advertisements: "How can it be good for me if it tastes nice?" But the psalmist is *not* saying "worship God, even if you find it distasteful; it will do you good anyway." No, he is actually speaking about a discovery he has made, that worship is a *delight* to him. The truth of the matter is that he finds it to be thrilling, as well as his duty.

You can sense this both in the *way* he writes (the psalm pulsates with life and joy) and in *what* he writes (the psalm also pulsates with devotion to God!). This ordinary man becomes someone extraordinary as he praises God. He becomes poet, chorister, composer, musician, theologian, all in one! He sings (verse 1); he makes melody (verse 3); he is glad (verse 4). His whole being seems to be taken up into this grand activity.

What has happened to him (and what happens to us in worship) is that he has discovered his destiny. He was made for this, as the famous first question of the Westminster *Shorter Catechism* says: "*What is the chief end of man?* Man's chief end is to *glorify* God, and to *enjoy* Him forever." It is only when we are restored to God, and begin to worship Him, that instead of falling short of His glory through sin (Romans 3:23), we begin to see His glory, by grace, and bow joyfully and willingly before Him.

This is why, every time we meet in Christian worship, we ought to have a sense of sharing in the powers of the world to come (Hebrews 6:5). It is the explanation of why, in praise and worship, we are sometimes conscious of another world altogether, a better, more glorious, heavenly world— as we find ourselves in a special sense in the presence of God. At last we have found our destiny there!

Savior, if of Zion's city
    I through grace a member am,
Let the world deride or pity,
    I will glory in Thy name:
Fading is the worldling's pleasure,
    All his boasted pomp and show;
Solid joys and lasting treasure
    None but Zion's children know.

(John Newton)

+   +   +

The third element of worship described in Psalm 92 is *the nature of worship*. What is it? The whole psalm tells us. But there is an expression used in it, synonymous with worship, that is especially striking. It is the verb *proclaim* (verses 2,15). Worship is proclamation; notice that. Worship *includes* proclamation, of course. But notice that, for this man, worship *is* proclamation.

Obviously in some churches proclamation, or preaching, is a major element in worship services. But more than that is in view here. The psalmist sees every element in worship as an opportunity "to proclaim your love in the morning and your faithfulness at night" (verse 2). And he sees that at the end of their lives the elderly (too frail to proclaim by preaching!) still "stay fresh and green, proclaiming, 'the LORD is upright; he is my Rock'" (verses 14-15).

Perhaps a better word to use would be *acclaim*. In our worship we are acclaiming God, and exclaiming because of what we know Him to be in His grace and power. That is why the Psalms are full of such expressions as, "shout to God with cries of joy" (Psalm 47:1); "Shout with joy to God, all the earth!" (Psalm 66:1); "Shout for joy to the LORD, all the earth" (Psalm 98:4). The proclamation of God includes teaching and preaching (and worship depends upon it to give it substance and strength); but it also involves our songs, our prayers, and indeed the very spirit in which we come together with a desire for the Lord to have the center stage in all that we do.

One beautiful expression of this spirit in Psalm 92 is in the words, "How great are your works, O LORD, how profound your thoughts!" (verse 5). It seems as though the very act of proclaiming all that God had done overwhelmed the psalmist with a new sense of the privilege of worship, and instinctively he let out these words of awe and wonder. His experience is like that of Isaiah—who spoke to others of the holiness of God, and then, in the Temple, heard the haunting melody of Heaven's seraphim, as they called to one another in the presence of the Holy God: "Holy"; and then, perhaps moved once more by what they saw Him to be: "Holy"; and then, again, "Holy is the LORD Almighty, the whole earth is full of his glory" (Isaiah 6:3).

Have you ever tasted worship that takes place in the presence of God, like that? It produces holy awe, and enables us to experience and understand the words of Habakkuk 2:20: "The LORD is in his holy temple; let all the earth be silent before him."

Paul says that when we sing praises we make

melody to the Lord in our hearts, and we also instruct one another (Colossians 3:16). It is in these truths, and for this purpose, that we do so. We certainly live in an age when that kind of instruction is sorely needed.

> Before Jehovah's awesome throne,
>> Ye nations, bow with sacred joy:
> Know that the Lord is God alone;
>> He can create, and He destroy.
>
> His sovereign power, without our aid,
>> Made us of clay, and formed us men;
> And when like wandering sheep we strayed,
>> He brought us to His fold again.
>
> We'll crowd Thy gates with thankful songs;
>> High as the heavens our voices raise;
> And earth, with her ten thousand tongues,
>> Shall fill Thy courts with sounding praise.

What a glorious vision for true worship!

+ + +

The final dimension of worship described in Psalm 92 is, *the fruit of worship.* Does worship really make a difference? It does—for the simple reason that the most significant factor in the life of God's people is *how they think about God;* and how we think about God is profoundly influenced by our proclamation of God in worship and our acclamation of Him in praise.

The writer of Psalm 92 knew what it was to

face difficulties and bitter opposition. What gave him stability in the face of the apparent prosperity of evil men was his knowledge that God was their judge. It was through his deepening consciousness of God's power and victory over his enemies that he realized he had nothing to fear from them.

There is a similar lesson taught by Asaph in Psalm 73. He tells us that he had almost given up his faith because of the prosperity and apparent immunity of wicked men. But then he went into the Temple, and—presumably through the worship and praise, the reading and proclamation—then he "understood their final destiny" (Psalm 73:17). He realized that his own view was time-bound and short-sighted. But in the presence of the eternal God, and in the consciousness of His glory, Asaph saw his own life and the life of the world in a different perspective—God's perspective!

So too, in Psalm 92, in the face of opposition, the psalmist finds new stability in his life. He receives strength from God ("You have exalted my horn like that of a wild ox," verse 10); he sees the wisdom of God which the foolish man can never grasp (verses 5-7); he appreciates the permanent blessing that God's children experience, so that even in old age (and especially in old age!) "they will still bear fruit. . . . they will stay fresh and green, proclaiming, 'The LORD is upright; he is my Rock'" (verses 14-15). And all because God's people are "planted in the house of the LORD" (verse 13).

It is at the end of life, not only at the begin-

ning, that Christians are most different from the
rest of the world. Then the true beauty of a
woman, the true character of a man, is seen for
what it really is. That is why there sometimes
seems to be a touch of glory and light about the
lives of elderly Christians. They have remained
"fresh and green" as Psalm 92 suggests, because
their hearts have been given to the Lord in worship. As Newton said, the worldling's pleasure is
fading; it is just "pomp and show." But the wor-
shiper of God, in Spirit and truth, knows joys that
are solid, and treasures that are lasting!

True worship puts character into our lives,
humility into our bearing, strength and confidence into our witnessing. But will it still remain
"the missing jewel of the evangelical church"? Let
us learn to worship God, with the faithfulness and
joy of the author of Psalm 92. Let us become "the
kind of worshipers the Father seeks" (John 4:23).

11
Remember The Lord

The man or woman who has a heart for God will be someone who is determined to remember the Lord.

Somewhere along the line, the idea of being a *decisive* and *determined* Christian has lost out in the fashion stakes. We have let the world squeeze us into its mold. For there, in the world, the idea of *permanent* commitment is rare indeed, either in employment or in marriage. Nowadays we cannot promise anything. Curiously we have become so self-effacing that we are no longer sure whether or not we will keep the promises we make! But *will* is the operative word, for promises of the most solemn nature are broken today because of a lack of willpower and determination. It is not really that "times have changed." We have changed. "Strong" twentieth-century man has a flabby will, a delinquent level of commitment, and an almost neurotic fear of anything that smacks of holiness or righteousness. The tragedy is that the spirit of the age has infected the people of God's new age, in the Church. Sometimes we cover our failure over with theology (of all things!)—we know ourselves too well to promise very much to God! But that is bad theology. It is also bad spirituality. For God calls us to promise ourselves to Him in a lifelong commitment of faithfulness and obedience. He does not regard our failure here as a becoming modesty, or an understandable reticence. He has other names for it: *disobedience, disloyalty, backsliding, faithlessness.*

Our spiritual forefathers recognized this disposition in their own hearts, but determined to have "hearts for God"; they made every effort to overcome and conquer it. That is why their diaries would sometimes contain *vows,* or *covenants* they would make to the Lord. In His presence they would commit themselves, by His grace, to remember Him and to live the whole of their lives before Him.

In our study of what it means to know God and to have a heart set on following Him, we have come to the point where we, too, must face this issue squarely. Do you have the resolution to vow to the Lord that, in a new way, you will remember Him? If the knowledge of God is to be anything more to you than an intellectual pastime, you need to do this. It is part of your *worship* of God. The praise we are to give Him includes the praise of a life that fulfills the vow to serve Him (Psalm 65:1). Yielding yourself—deliberately, intelligently—to the Lord is part of your worship (Romans 12:1-2).

When Moses looked back on the events that had fulfilled the promise God gave him at the burning bush, he set before the people the response that the Lord expected from them: "Be careful not to forget the Lord, and to observe his commands." There, in a sentence, is the true response to the discovery of God's character revealed in all that He says and does. Do not "forget" Him. Live in His presence, and open the whole of your life to His will expressed in His Word ("observe his commands").

God's people—then, as now—were plagued by spiritual amnesia. That is why, along with his exhortation, Moses spoke to them with great force about the influences causing it, the repercussions of its presence in their lives, and the only remedy that would sustain and cure them.

+   +   +

The cause of spiritual amnesia is usually twofold. First, *we fail to profit from the Lord's past activity in our lives.* Moses put it well in his context:

> Remember how the LORD your God led you all the way in the desert these forty years, to humble you and to test you in order to know what was in your heart, whether or not you would keep his commands. He humbled you, causing you to hunger and then feeding you with

manna, which neither you nor your fathers had
known, to teach you that man does not live on
bread alone, but on every word that comes from
the mouth of the LORD. Your clothes did not
wear out and your feet did not swell during
these forty years. Know then in your heart that
as a man disciplines his son, so the LORD your
God disciplines you.

(Deuteronomy 8:2-5)

These are very significant and important
words. Their importance is underlined for us by
the fact that Jesus was especially familiar with
them and had obviously committed them to
memory. He used them as part of His spiritual
armor against the temptations of the Devil (when
He was in the wilderness being tested—Matthew
4:4—as the Israelites were).

God had been gracious to the Israelites. He
had been the God He promised He would be: He
saved them, led them, protected them, provided
for them (no swollen feet in forty years!). Yet, they
were in danger of taking all this for granted. They
saw a desert, and old clothes, and manna in the
wilderness. But they did not have the eyes *to see
what God was doing through these experiences.*
Moses says God was trying to *humble* them, to
teach them, and to *educate* and *discipline* them as a
Father. But they did not see what God was doing;
they learned nothing, and rather than being stimulated to praise and fellowship with God, they
became indifferent to Him.

Reflect, for a moment, on your past. Did it

once fill you with a sense of excitement and thanks-giving that God had brought you to Himself, had set you free to serve and love Him? Did you once gratefully trace the steps by which you came to Christ, the different ways in which God taught you, the people He brought your way and through whom He molded you into what you are now?

Do you still reflect back on God's grace in your life? Are you still conscious that being a Christian means experiencing the living touch of God on your daily life? Or have you, like the Israelites, failed to profit from the Lord's activity? Now life simply "happens," events and experi-ences come and go, almost indistinguishably. You no longer see the Lord's hand at work. You no longer sense yourself to be the child of a Father who is always teaching you, always disciplining you for His own glory.

The forgetfulness of the Hebrews is appar-ently a recurring syndrome for Christian "He-brews" as well. Later, in the New Testament, we come across the same symptoms, and the Chris-tians need to be told, "In your struggle against sin, you have not yet resisted to the point of shedding your blood. And you have forgotten that word of encouragement that addresses you as sons: 'My son, do not make light of the Lord's discipline, and do not lose heart when he rebukes you, because the Lord disciplines those he loves, and he punishes everyone he accepts as a son'" (Hebrews 12:4-6, quoting Proverbs 3:11-12). Here Old Testament and New Testament experience are the same. The writer recognized a diminishing level of commitment to holiness on the one hand, coupled with a forgetfulness of God's Word and a blindness to God's activity on the other. Is that dismal plane of experience where you and I are?

+   +   +

The second cause of spiritual amnesia is *the existence of a proud heart in response to the Lord's liberality*. Moses speaks frankly about this, too:

> When you have eaten and are satisfied, praise the LORD your God for the good land he has given you. Be careful that you do not forget the LORD your God, failing to observe his commands, his laws and his decrees that I am giving you this day. Otherwise, when you eat and are satisfied, when you build fine houses and settle down, and when your herds and flocks grow large and your silver and gold increase and all you have is multiplied, then your heart will become proud and you will forget the LORD your God, who brought you out of Egypt, out of the land of slavery. He led you through the vast and dreadful desert, that thirsty and waterless land, with its venomous snakes and scorpions. He brought you water out of hard rock. He gave you manna to eat in the desert, something your fathers had never known, to humble and to test you so that in the end it might go well with you. You may say to yourself, "My power and the strength of my hands have produced this wealth for me." But remember the LORD your God, for it is he who gives you the ability to produce

wealth, and so confirms his covenant, which he
swore to your forefathers, as it is today. (Deuteronomy 8:10-18)

You would hardly believe that God's people
could receive so much so clearly from the Lord,
and still become proud of their own activity—
unless you were acquainted with the deceitfulness
of your own heart. But those who do know their
own hearts recognize how easily each of us may fall
into the sin of pride and self-sufficiency, when
God intends us to be humble and learn that our
sufficiency depends upon Him.

Have affluence and prosperity proved to be a
snare in your life? Jesus spoke of this danger in His
parable of the Sower and the soils. Some soil failed
to produce fruit because of the presence of thorns,
which Jesus interpreted to be "the worries of this
life, the deceitfulness of wealth and the desires for
other things" which come in, choke the seed of
God's Word, and make it unfruitful (Mark 4:18-
19). God provides all we need, but we become
obsessed by the gift rather than the Giver, and
soon we think of His "gifts" as our "rights"
because we have earned them or deserved them.
More and more we secretly desire to write across
our lives, "I did it my way." And as a consequence
we distance ourselves from the Lord, become
insensitive to Him, and forget His grace.

This turning away from God, as we noticed in
chapter eight, was what happened to King Uzziah:
"He sought God during the days of Zechariah,
who instructed him in the fear of God. As long as

170 Remember The Lord

he sought the LORD, God gave him success. . . .
His fame spread far and wide, for he was greatly
helped until he became powerful. But after Uzziah
became powerful, his pride led to his downfall. He
was unfaithful to the LORD" (2 Chronicles 26:5,
15-16). It was not his power, nor his success, that
destroyed his spiritual usefulness, but his forgetfulness, his failure to remember the Lord, and his
consequent unfaithfulness.

Prosperity is a gift. It can be a blessing; *it is
always a test*. That was what Moses urged the
people to realize. Both adversity and prosperity
have that function in our Christian lives. They test
whether or not we have a commitment to the Lord
that will help us see both those experiences in
relation to Him. All Christians encounter one or
the other. Most of us have regularly experienced
both. Did you pass the test? Did your experience
draw you closer to the Lord as you committed
your way to Him? Or did you, like the Israelites,
forget Him and become wrapped up in yourself—
in either your problems or your achievements?

Will you face up to these issues, and make a
fresh vow to the Lord that, with His help, through
His grace, you will not go on forgetting Him?

The seriousness of these issues compelled
Moses to tell the Israelites not only about the
causes, but also about the *consequences* of spiritual
amnesia. He realized what they had forgotten, that
the nature of their relationship to God was such
that their spiritual sickness was serious and could
indeed be a terminal condition, because they were
God's covenanted people.

At first glance this seems contradictory, for Moses speaks about God confirming His covenant (Deuteronomy 8:18). But this is precisely the point. God always confirms His covenant. He always keeps the vows He has made to His people. But what precisely is His covenant? It is the sworn promise that those who trust Him will enter into all the riches of His blessing. But the corollary of this promise is that those who are unfaithful to His covenant will discover they have rejected His blessing. Their hardness of heart will lead to judgment and loss. So, says Moses:

> The LORD did not set his affection on you and choose you because you were more numerous than other peoples, for you were the fewest of all peoples. But it was because the LORD loved you and kept the oath he swore to your forefathers that he brought you out with a mighty hand and redeemed you from the land of slavery, from the power of Pharaoh king of Egypt. Know therefore that the LORD your God is God; he is the faithful God, keeping his covenant of love to a thousand generations of those who love him and keep his commands. But
> > those who hate him he will repay to their face by destruction;
> he will not be slow to repay to their face those who hate him.
>
> (Deuteronomy 7:7-10)

This is the way in which covenant faithfulness inevitably operates. We find this very clearly expressed in Hebrews, which has sometimes been called "The Epistle of the Covenant." On several occasions its author warns us not to fall into the unbelief and failure of the people of God in the days of the Exodus: "See to it, brothers, that none of you has a sinful, unbelieving heart that turns away from the living God. But encourage one another daily, as long as it is called Today, so that none of you may be hardened by sin's deceitfulness. We have come to share in Christ *if* we hold firmly till the end the confidence we had at first. As has just been said: 'Today, if you hear his voice, do not harden your hearts as you did in the rebellion'" (Hebrews 3:12-15; see also the whole series of "warning passages" that punctuate Hebrews: 2:1-3; 4:1-2,11; 10:26-31).

This is the measure of God's commitment to His covenant: He will remain faithful to it, *whatever the consequences may be.* That is why the self-satisfaction that leads to spiritual forgetfulness is so deceitful and so deadly. As a result, the promised blessing of God is refused, and we fall under His judgment.

The solemn truth of the gospel is that, in spiritual things, you get what you set your heart on. Set your heart on knowing God and He will reveal Himself through His Word; set your heart on serving Him and you will not lack the opportunity to do so. But set your heart on nothing of spiritual consequence, and that is precisely what you will receive—*nothing of spiritual consequence.* Set your heart on your own ambitions, and they will, very likely, be fulfilled. Yet more solemn,

God may give you your heart's desire. He did exactly that for His people in the wilderness. He saved them for His own sake and glory, and led them through the desert, yet "they soon forgot what he had done and did not wait for his counsel. In the desert they gave in to their craving; in the wasteland they put God to the test. *So he gave them what they asked for,* but sent a wasting disease upon them" (Psalm 106:13-15). All that, despite Moses' warning to them:

> If you ever forget the LORD your God and fol-
> low other gods and worship and bow down to
> them, I testify against you today that you will
> surely be destroyed. Like the nations the LORD
> destroyed before you, so you will be destroyed
> for not obeying the LORD your God. (Deuter-
> onomy 8:19-20)

Think for a moment about where your life has led you thus far. What ambitions and aspirations have been fulfilled? Has the Lord given you many of the things you longed for—materially, person-ally, socially, professionally? But now, meditate on this: *Do you have the Lord Himself with these things, or do you have them without Him?* Have you forgotten the Lord?

+ + +

Moses spoke to the people in these terms because he was their pastor. He was deeply concerned for them. Remember his prayer: "Please forgive their sin—but if not, then blot me out of the book you have written"—(Exodus 32:32). He did not warn them about the importance of remembering the Lord without also indicating to them how their spiritual amnesia could be cured. He mentioned two essentials.

First, *a heart wholly satisfied with the Lord's provision keeps us fresh and eager to remember and serve Him.* Several times during this one section of his long exposition and application of God's law, Moses had underlined how God had given the people everything they ever needed. When there had been any lack He had supplied it fully and consistently (see Deuteronomy 8:3-4,7,10,15-16, 18). The past, the present, and the future were all in God's hands. He would never leave them or fail them. What they needed to do was to see that what God gave—no more and no less—was a perfect supply. Here was an issue they had failed to resolve—would they rest content with God's wisdom, grace, and sovereign provision, or would they always insist on taking matters into their own hands?

The story of the Exodus is both historical and typical. It happened, in history; but it was also meant by God as an object lesson, an illustration of the final provision He would make for His people through Jesus Christ. That is why, particularly in Matthew's Gospel, there is so much about the life and ministry of Jesus that is patterned on the Exodus. For Christ is now God's provision for us. In Him, says Paul, God has given us every spiritual blessing (Ephesians 1:3). All the treasures of wisdom and knowledge are stored up for His people in Him (Colossians 2:3). God gave Him for us all, and thus assures us that He will give us everything in Christ (Romans 8:32). But, the issue is: *Are you satisfied with God's provision?* Have you learned contentment with what He adds to your life, and the gifts He has given you, or do you hanker for what Jesus called "the desires for other things" (Mark 4:19)?

The other essential cure for spiritual amnesia is *a heart wholly submitted to the Lord's will.* Notice that many of the exhortations Moses issued to the people have to do with *heart* and *will:* "be careful to follow," "remember," "observe" may all seem to be connected with the mind, the memory, the understanding. But actually they are all intimately connected with our wills, because they all have to do with *submission to God's Word.* What God was concerned about was to see "whether or not you would keep his commands" (Deuteronomy 8:2). This concern is not that of a despot; it is the intimate concern of a father. He humbled and tested His children, "that in the end it might go well" with them (Deuteronomy 8:16). That is His deepest desire: He longs for His children to submit their hearts and wills to His will, because only then can they discover the blessing He plans to provide in His way and at His time.

Have you vowed to submit to the Lord? In the last analysis, that is what it means to remember Him.

William Booth, the founder of the Salvation Army movement in the nineteenth century, was once asked about the secret of his spiritual power.

He gave an interesting and illuminating reply: "There was a day in my life when I vowed that God would have everything there was to have of William Booth." Years after his death, his daughter was reminded by a friend of what General Booth had vowed. She said: "You know, the vow on its own wasn't the real secret of father's life. The real secret was that *he kept it*."

If we are to have a heart that is devoted to the Lord, we need to make the same vow. Make that vow in response to what we have discovered together about God. Then you will know what it is to have *a heart for God.*

> *The goal is God Himself*
> *Not joy, nor peace;*
> *Not even blessing,*
> *But Himself, my God.*
> *'Tis His to lead me there,*
> *Not mine, but His—*
> *At any cost, dear Lord,*
> *By any road.*